Answers From the
Angels
A Book of Angel Letters

Other Books
by Terry Lynn Taylor

Messengers of Light:
The Angels' Guide to Spiritual Growth
Guardians of Hope:
The Angels' Guide to Personal Growth

Answers From the
Angels
A Book of Angel Letters

by
Terry Lynn Taylor
and
Friends

H J Kramer Inc
Tiburon, California

H J Kramer Inc
P.O. Box 1082
Tiburon, CA 94920

Editor: Nancy Grimley Carleton
Illustrations: Marty Noble
Cover Art: Raphael, c. 1513, Sistine Madonna (detail)
Cover Design: Spectra Media
Composition: Classic Typography
Book Production: Schuettge and Carleton
Manufactured in the United States of America.
10 9 8 7 6 5 4 3 2 1

Raphael painting:
Courtesy of
Gemäldegalerie, Dresden,
Erich Lessing, Art Resources, N.Y.

Library of Congress Cataloging-in-Publication Data

Taylor, Terry Lynn, 1955–
    Answers from the angels : a book of angel letters / Terry Lynn
Taylor.
        p.   cm.
    Includes bibliographical references.
    ISBN 0-915811-43-X : $9.95
    1. Angels – Miscellanea.   2. Taylor, Terry Lynn, 1955–   Messengers
of light.   3. Taylor, Terry Lynn, 1955–   Guardians of hope.
I. Title.
BL477.T374   1993
291.2'15 – dc20   92-37124
                                                                              CIP

This book is dedicated to all of the
people I have met through the mail.
I honor your freedom of expression. May
the angels bless you with grace, creativity,
and continued divine inspiration.

T.L.T.

To Our Readers

*The books we publish are our
contribution to an emerging world
based on cooperation rather than on
competition, on affirmation of the human
spirit rather than on self-doubt, and on the
certainty that all humanity is connected.
Our goal is to touch as many lives as
possible with a message of hope
for a better world.*

Hal and Linda Kramer, Publishers

Contents

Preface

Angels are very sweet. They guide you day and night. One mysterious thing is, there isn't one in sight. Angels are messengers from God. They go to people who are sad and try to make them happy. For people who are already happy, angels make them stay that way.

I think angels look like beautiful creatures with wings, and they fly around. In case you don't know, you and I have angels by our side every second of the day, telling our conscience what's right and what's wrong. These angels are called "guardian angels."

Elizabeth Ann Godfrey (Age 11)
Colorado

Hope and inspiration come to me in the mail almost every day. People from all over the world have written in response to a request I put in the back of my first book about angels, *Messengers of Light,* where I asked for angel experiences, poetry, and angel requests. The letters I have received allow me to view a side of life that warms my heart and plays music to my soul, a side we don't always get to read about in the newspapers or see on the evening news. These letters are meant to be shared. The angels move us to share our blessed experiences, allowing us to promote angelic ideals on this planet that may help other humans on their path.

Reading about angel experiences helps us strengthen our own angel consciousness and lets us know we are not alone. We come to realize that the angels are with us, and so are other people of "like mind." Besides describing the ways angels interact with humans, the writers of the letters can teach us many other important things. Some letter writers share techniques and practices that make their lives flow and that strengthen their personal angelic ideals and spirituality. I receive letters from true philosophers. According to the *Oxford American Dictionary*, philosophy is the search for understanding of the basic truths and principles of the universe, of life, of morals, and of human perception. These letter writers may not call themselves philosophers, but almost everyone who searches for truth on the spiritual path is a philosopher. Glimpsing into the philosophies of our fellow humans can enlighten and inspire us. Looking into how people think and feel spiritually shows us that, although we are all unique in our thinking, there are also many ways in which we are similar and connected. From reading about other people's spiritual experiences, we also learn that we are all teachers for one another. We can each promote angel consciousness in our own special way.

Angels are messengers of the highest divine energy in the universe—God. The angels do not want to be worshiped, and this is important to remember. The joy angels bring to us is a gift from God. The angels are our spiritual helpers; they want to help us live in accordance with the highest divine principles in the universe. K. Martin-Kuri, a well-known angelologist (an angel expert), warns us that "angels should never be treated as personal slaves nor as substitutes for God. Rather, they should always be seen as God's servants, 'local representatives of the management,' who deserve appreciation rather than worship." Martin-Kuri also mentions that angels have been ignored and rarely thanked for all the work they do for humans. I think this is changing; as you will see in the letters, people express gratitude when they are touched by the angels.

Some common themes emerge as messages from the angels:

We are not alone.

We are protected.

Everything is going to be okay.

This, too, shall pass.

Take a break and have a laugh.

Lighten up and take things less seriously; by so doing, you will experience more clarity and creativity in life—and much more fun!

The spiritual path is one of lightness and joy.

It is not easy to follow a spiritual path in a world where darkness and misery abound.

The love and joy of the angels are always available to light our way and bring heartfelt meaning into our lives.

Life can still be wonderful and joyful, no matter how dark the rest of the world seems.

Remember what Anne Frank said while living under horrendous conditions, during one of the darkest times in history: "In spite of everything, I still believeve that people are really good at heart." People really *are* good at heart; I am reminded of this truth each time I open my "angel mail."

The angels teach us to carry the peace of God—true mental peace—out into the world. We learn not to get upset over trivial issues. If we have to wait in line or drive behind a slow car in traffic, we begin to understand that perhaps this delay is saving us from something bad that could have happened had we rushed and pushed our way through. By leaving home with the peace of God and the angels within us, we create a pattern of magic in the universe, and we are rewarded in the most meaningful ways. When life becomes meaningful, it becomes priceless, worth living to the fullest. As you read these letters, you will see how the angels help us find meaning in our lives.

I chose the letters for this book by heart feeling. What I mean is that I sensed that particular letters would reach people at important times – that readers might be having experiences similiar to the ones described in the letters and gain an awareness about how the angels could assist them. Other letters might inspire readers to proceed with creative projects they haven't yet found the courage to start. If a letter really moves you, empower yourself and the person who wrote it by saying thank-you to the angels for their help and inspiration; then thank God. Savor the letters written for you, by you, and about your invisible helpers – the angels. Read a letter a day. Share the letters in your angel study groups. Enjoy being part of the human family – the children of God.

About the Letters

Most of the letters I have received are in response to *Messengers of Light.* Other letter writers are responding to a newsletter I put out at the beginning of each season entitled *Angels Can Fly.* For instance, you may notice people writing to me about signs, wonders, synchronisms, and so forth. They were responding to newsletter discussions of these ideas.

Please read the letters with an open mind. If an opinion is expressed that differs from one you hold, get used to the idea that there are no "right" or "wrong" opinions – only opinions that are different or similar. There are no right or wrong religions, no right or wrong ways to God. When we step onto a spiritual path with the honest intention of using our free will to love God, even if we are sidetracked along the way, we will eventually take the turn on our path that leads us upward to transcend our human struggles and view the big picture. If something doesn't sit right with you, simply think of it as food for thought.

All of the letters are used with permission, and names and places appear the way each writer requested. Letters have been gently edited, with love, for style and clarity. The following poem captures the essence of angel letters.

Bea Rowley
Victoria, British Columbia, Canada

Angel Letters

Angel letters are the most
Exciting kind of "airmail" post—
As delicate as flakes of snow,
A merry nudge to let you know
That just around the edge of sight
Your world is full of rainbow light
And angel joy, and you're invited
To be aware, inspired, delighted
With angel news you might have missed.
They have you on their mailing list.

Acknowledgments

This book was coauthored by many angels. So, first, I thank all the angels who inspired the letter writers to write to me. I really don't know how I could say thank-you enough to the letter writers themselves for the blessings they have brought to my life. I feel honored and privileged to receive such love and wisdom in the mail each day. All of the writers who offered their letters to this book did so in the spirit of the angels. All were willing to share their personal experiences so that they could reach others who might need hope at an uncertain time in their lives. I have been overwhelmed by the kindness and generosity of each person who contributed to this book, and I am grateful to each one of you.

For the production and development of this book, I extend heartfelt gratitude to the following individuals: To my publishers, Hal and Linda Kramer, for taking special interest in the concept of this book and giving me another chance to share the wondrous blessings the angels give freely. To Linda, for sharing one of her angel experiences in this book, which became the cornerstone for Chapter 8, Animal Angels and Pets. To Nancy Grimley Carleton, of Berkeley, California, for her loving and gentle editing skills. I thank her for taking the time to write a special letter for Chapter 8. I know many people will be comforted by her contribution. To Tim Gunns, for his moral support, love, and encouragement, which helped to center me many times during the development of this book. His love has enriched my life and my creativity in many ways. To my family, for their unconditional love, humor, and strength. Especially to my sister Kathy,

Acknowledgments

for her moral support during the earthquake episodes. To Shannon Boomer and Linda Hayden, for their unconditional friendship and their contributions to the book. To Shannon, for her invaluable feedback on an early version of the manuscript. To Kathy Faulstich, Cheri Leslie, Uma Ergil, Bill Sotelo, Pierre Jovanovic, Suzanna Solomon, K. Martin-Kuri, Lori Jean Flory, Sol Ta Triane, Elizabeth Ann Godfrey, Beverly Hale-Watson, Cher Jung, Joan Wilen, Lydia Wilen, Larayne Gordon, and Pam Watson, for their special support of this book and for their devotion to increasing angel awareness. "No person is a failure who has friends!"

Angel Introductions

1

Angels take root in our consciousness the moment we establish a connection. We each have a guardian angel who has always been with us, so in essence we have always been connected to the angels, especially in our heart and soul. Angel consciousness is something more; it begins when we become fully aware of the angels around us and the possibilities and wonders they bring to our lives. Establishing a personal connection with the angels is a simple process. You don't even have to say you believe *in angels. Just begin by allowing yourself to be open to the ways of the angels, and you will notice all the wonderful happenings the angels promote around you. Then you won't need to* believe; *you will simply* know.

After you have become "angel conscious," you will want to communicate with the angels in your own special way. Some people simply converse with the angels as if they were sitting in the room with a friend. Others write letters to the angels. When the angels communicate with us, it is mostly through inspiration and little signs. They may bring us humor in a dark moment. Or they may help us notice a wonderful coincidence, or synchronism, to let us know all is well. In some of the letters, people mention ANGEL® cards. The ANGEL® cards consist of a deck of fifty-two small cards, with a picture of an angel doing something and one word on each one. The words include Joy, Clarity, Synthesis, and Creativity. For details on where to order ANGEL® cards, see my note to readers at the end of the book.

Because we are all unique beings, we express our connection to the angels in unique ways. In this section you will see some of the wonders angels bring to us when we first welcome them into our lives as cocreators of our destiny. Sometimes the angels actually materialize a gift to let us know they are with us.

Shannon
Venice, California

A few years ago I had just come through a long period of depression that resulted in dissolving my marriage of ten years. I guess I hadn't realized the tremendous burdens of the relationship, or its lack of spiritual basis, until it was over, when I experienced a most astonishing renewal of innocence and faith in God. There is nothing to compare with the beautiful gift of innocence. I will be forever grateful and in love with God for the freedom from guilt and the burden of blaming myself. It was during this period that I began to know the presence of angels.

It is difficult to describe the sweetness of the way angels ministered to me then. They were healing my heart with a profound subtlety, and I was blossoming from the inside out with joy and hope for the future; physically, I was beginning to look much younger, and emotionally I was demonstrating stamina unknown to me before.

My powerful feelings of gratitude moved me to pray constantly. But in my spiritual immaturity, I asked for things that were better left unanswered. No matter; I was in such grace during this period that the angels would send me gifts to console me and let me know I was not alone.

On one such occasion, my son Gideon and I were driving down the main street leading to our home. Looking ahead toward the corner where we lived, I saw a flash of gold on the street. It took a few seconds to register in my mind, but then I stopped the car in the middle of the street, just where we turned onto our street. I opened the door and looked down to see – just within my reach without my having to undo my seat belt – a golden angel statue lying on her side. I swept her up, and in my glee I shouted. Gideon was all flushed and amazed, with wide eyes and open mouth.

We hurried home and rushed in the house to look at her. On close examination, we saw she was carefully sculpted on her knees in the repose of prayer. The bottoms of her bare feet showed delicate and lovely. She had a golden gown wrapped around her small body. In a word, she was beautiful – and hand painted in Italy.

A few months later, the golden angel appeared again. I left the house early to be at a bookstore when it opened. When I got there, it wasn't open yet, and during the night someone had broken out the plate-glass window. In the bookstore's haste to board up the window, they moved various estate-sale objects to another window. I noticed a cluster of statues very symbolically significant to the people closest to me in my life. This interested me, so I went home to get my camera. A few days later when I got the pictures back, I noticed that between Abraham Lincoln and a goddess statue appeared the lovely, solid-gold profile of an angel.

Since then, my angel experiences have changed. They are not quite so materialistically spectacular, not as concrete, but the honeymoon with God I was given during that time changed me and permanently reassured me of the presence of love, goodness, and mercy.

Jeff Boutel

Washington

I've been on a singular, upward path for eighteen years. I am now thirty-six, so that's half my life, which has passed at the speed of light. I am a man compelled—drawn. I have no choice but to seek truth.

At the end of your workshop, when you asked everyone to pick an ANGEL® card, I picked the card with the word *Grace* on it. I assumed *Grace* referred to "God's Grace." But two days later, I was awakened by the most compelling thought: Grace is the name of my guardian angel.

The next day, when I went to collect my mail, guess what I found? A postcard with the word *Grace* printed on the front. On the back was a beautiful handwritten love poem, which was signed "Grace." Now the interesting thing is, I have no friends or acquaintances by the name of Grace. In fact, I've never met anyone named Grace—until now. I've no doubt my guardian angel was sending me a very clear message.

Christy Schafer

North Carolina

Oh, by the way, the day after I started asking the angels for guidance, two beautiful poems showed up in my mailbox. One was on being human and the other was written by a seventy-eight-year-old woman stating what she would do differently if she had her life to live over again. I have asked all the people I know if they put the poems in my mailbox, and they all say no. What a riot. I am still laughing!

Loraine
Winnipeg, Manitoba, Canada

My friend picked me up, and we went to pick up your book for her and a deck of ANGEL® cards for me. In the store, my friend took the cards out and spread them facedown on the counter. I said to her and the owner of the store that love was the ultimate answer and if we could give out love to all, what a wonderful world we would have.

My friend laughed and said, "You can't pick out the angel card you want; you have to be happy with the angel card that you get." I said, "Oh no, it's love, that's where it's at, it's the one thing He asked of us." Then I drew my ANGEL® card, and the card I drew was Love. My friend just stared, her mouth open, and the owner smiled knowingly. I felt very peaceful.

Ana Rodriguez
Texas

One time I was trying to make a decision in my career. I felt very composed. It was a weekend, and when I woke up I went to the kitchen to make coffee. I noticed a little heart-shaped stone on the counter. I thought my son had brought it in, because we are always collecting pieces of nature that we feel have special energy. I asked him if he had found it for me, and he said no. Then I asked my life partner and got another no. Nobody else had been visiting that day.

I knew the stone was an answer from my angels telling me that they loved me and that I had made the right decision and that I must love myself and be okay with it. It is incredible that the stone is exactly in a heart shape.

I am the receptionist in my company, and every day people come to my desk to get their ANGEL® card for the day. I can see the difference in their attitude and energy because of the angels! The news has spread over the company that "angels give you messages in the reception area." People are getting the idea that to start the day in a positive way, with positive feelings, they can come to see what the angels have to say.

Barb Martin

Wisconsin

I gave a set of ANGEL® cards to a friend, and she chooses an angel each day. She has had a rather difficult time in the past with forgiveness of others. Well, one day she picked the card Forgiveness. She said she didn't "want" that angel for the day, so she put it back in the bowl and tried to choose again, and— guess what?—she got Forgiveness again! Well, to cut this short, she picked Forgiveness three more times before the angels "gave up for now." Too bad; I, too, feel that if she could forgive some past problems, she could move forward. The ANGEL® cards are great; Mirth, Abundance, Joy, and Love seem to spend a lot of time with us.

Linda Shields
New Jersey

Letter 1

I would like to make an angel request during a very troubled time. My husband has worked for the same company for eighteen years, and now we find out he will be laid off soon. Our lives are hanging in midair until we know when. We are hoping for a possible transfer. We need the strength and courage of Angel Michael and the guidance of any and all angels that can stand by us now.

Letter 2

Just to fill you in: My husband has found a job, and the angels have really been providing for us up until he started to work. I have two small businesses, which really picked up around the time of his layoff. My child-care business was great this summer, and I was able to bring in more children because of his being home. Whatever money we needed, God provided for us twofold.

I am the happiest I have ever been in my whole life, my marriage has remained strong and loving through all our trials, and my two children are healthy and happy. I thank God and the angels every day for all their blessings. Whenever I have doubts, a message from the angels always comes through. I really keep my eyes open now, and I'm always in awe of how many angels are with me every day.

Lauren Franciosi
Kentucky

I've had a very stressful two years with very little quality time for peace and meditation, which at one time I truly indulged in. My husband and I scheduled a week of "R & R" at a Bed and Breakfast that I had visited on a previous occasion, in a very peaceful and quiet town.

Prior to our journey, I was gathering up items to take on our trip. I felt a sudden, urgent need to work on a cross-stitch project I bought a year ago, titled "First Angel of Light." I didn't give it much thought. I also found right before the trip that I was *craving* angel food cake. I thought this was a strange craving, but again I didn't focus too much on it. On our drive we made a pit stop and popped into and out of a metaphysical bookstore. My husband was rather tired from our travels, and I said, "I won't be but five minutes." I was drawn immediately to where your book was located, and that was that. From then on, angels were popping up everywhere. In the room we had at the Bed and Breakfast, they had the most beautiful picture of an angel sleeping. A store I visited was having a clearance on angel items, so of course I stocked up!

P.S. We had a beautiful "dusting" of snow. Nothing icy – only pure white to accent nature sleeping. Someone once told me long ago that when it snows, the angels are having a pillow fight in heaven.

Wendy M.

Colorado

I've had a couple of noticeable angel experiences happen to me since I've opened myself up more to angels. I was thinking how nice it would be to receive a gift from my guardian angel, just to let me know that he was there listening to me. That very evening a friend of mine came to visit me after a day of Christmas shopping. She said that she had a gift for me, that when she'd seen it something just told her to buy it for me. It was a stained-glass angel. The gift itself was beautiful, but what thrilled me the most were the colors. The body of my winged gift is a beautiful emerald green, the head is an amber-gold, and the angel holds a harp of clear, etched glass. At the time, I was wearing an emerald green shirt, the light over my head had a yellow globe over it, and I was looking out the window. Am I reading too much into this gift from a very close and dear friend? If I am, that's okay—I won't give up!

Silvia Petersen-Gil Palacios

San Jose, California

I just finished reading your book *Messengers of Light,* and I really enjoyed it. Since then, I have welcomed angels into my life, and it is a great feeling! Now I understand that I was not that crazy when I was a little girl and used to make room in my chair so my angel could sit with me. It is when you grow up that people make you think that you are crazy, and then you stop believing; that is exactly the time when everything starts going wrong in life.

B. A. Kuczynski
Linden, New Jersey

Having experienced so many synchronisms, I choose to believe they are all "signs." I believe that virtually everything that happens to us is the opportunity for a learning experience. While I try not to get hung up on examining the deeper meaning of each event in my life, the angels have brought me a keener awareness of grace alive and working in my life, and of my potential for growth through this awareness. If we espouse the belief that the angels are with us constantly (and I do), then we must know that they are always trying to get through to us with messages designed to bring us into alignment with our higher selves. With each wonderful thing that happens to me, I look to God and the angels as the cause and try to determine what response I should make for the highest loving good of all concerned. When something "not so wonderful" occurs in my life, I no longer take it as a sign that I deserved punishment because I am a "not so wonderful" person; rather, I see it as a result of living in a world where we are not all seeking the same goal of enlightenment. I don't believe that we as mortals (humans) have the capacity to disappoint or hurt the angels or God, but I do believe that when we are not acting in accordance with our higher mission, they tend to back off and don't knock themselves out trying to get through to us.

12

Allan P. Duncan
Burlington, New Jersey

In response to your article in the newsletter on "signs and wonders," I must say that I've seen so many it would take a complete book just to record them! As I told you before, I see deer and red-tailed hawks frequently after prayer, meditation, or writing an angel letter. At first I just thought this was just a coincidence. Over time I knew this was a sign to let me know that everything was going to be okay. Whenever I see one now, I smile and thank my angel, Liara. I have learned to listen to the "still small voice within," and over time I have learned to trust my intuition. I know when something is a sign now. It's like the difference between faith and hope. In time you just *know* the validity of your beliefs, and hope is transformed into faith— something much more powerful than hope. When I'm in my spiritual flow, I don't *hope* that God will help me; I *know* that he is already here with all of his avatars and angels, and I am full of peace and serenity.

Beverly Hale Watson
North Carolina

While I don't "see" angels, I can feel when they are near. I also understand that God sends his messengers in many forms. A couple of weeks ago as I was working on my latest book, a very large hawk appeared on a tree limb directly in line to the window where I was sitting. He was big enough to feed four to five people. For four hours solid, he sat there, and then he flew off. We live on a wooded lot in a subdivision, and it amazed us that the hawk could maneuver around without catching his wings on the foliage.

My daughter Kay lives in New York, and she works with the gifts of the Holy Spirit as well. I mentioned to her what had taken place. Two days later she called with a message: "The eyes of the hawk are upon you; the Lord is always near." I asked her if the hawk would ever return. She replied "yes," and at that moment my husband and I turned and looked out the kitchen window and the hawk appeared. When Kay completed the information, the hawk departed. Our seeing of hawks has increased during this past year. Sometimes they appear out of nowhere and vanish, as if a magician said, "Poof."

One time my husband was given a gift of a glider ride. As the tow plane was pulling the glider up in the air to the proper altitude, a hawk flew over the cockpit and proceeded to ride the air current near the plane. The pilot couldn't believe what he was seeing, and my husband just smiled, knowing it was a sign that they were not alone on this flight. Yes, angels are among us, if we will only take notice of their presence!

Pierre Jovanovic
Paris, France/Malibu, California

In November 1990, my newspaper sent me to the United States to cover the Comdex Fall, the world's main computer and software exhibition in Las Vegas. I took a walk in this amazing city and discovered a chapel called Guardian Angel Cathedral. I went in to pray.

I was attracted to the chapel because some weeks before, hearing a French rock song about angels, I asked myself if I really did have a guardian angel the way my grandmother told me when I was a child. This question was funny to me. I imagined a guy with huge wings flying twenty-four hours per day behind me, following closer than my own shadow. It was a romantic idea, but definitely not serious, for a journalist in charge of the scientific and computing section of a widely distributed French newspaper. But I began to receive signs. In the cathedral I bought a little card with an angel pin on it. The card was the traditional religious prayer card of an angel taking care of two children crossing a bridge.

After leaving Guardian Angel Cathedral, I took a taxi cab back to my hotel, and the cab driver got lost. I ended up at a bookstore where I found *Messengers of Light*. I read it on a plane ride back to Los Angeles, city of the angels. In my hotel room, I took out the little guardian angel card and began to observe all the details. The angel was a beautiful red-headed young woman with an angelic face, long wavy hair, and two wonderful wings. It was funny to me because I never thought that my guardian angel would be a beautiful angel-woman, so joking to myself I said to the picture: "Look, if you're so beautiful, I'm ready to be married to you!" Two months later, I find myself in love with a fantastic red-headed French woman who makes me laugh all the time.

[TLT: Since Pierre wrote to me in December 1990, he has had many amazing angel experiences. Pierre and his red-headed angel,

*Carol, had a baby girl angel, Gabrielle, in October 1991. He also
ended up living in Malibu, near where I live, and we have become
friends who share deep spiritual experiences. The angels seem to be
leading us on similar paths.]*

Cristina Tanrozzi Laparé
Quebec, Canada

Your book was guided to me by my dearest friend – my
guardian angel. Somehow deep inside there was something I
was looking for that I couldn't identify. It was something I wanted
to express that was deep inside – a certain truth. Many hints were
given to me, but at the time I didn't catch the meaning, though
I would meditate.

Once a psychic told me, years ago, "You have symbolically
remained a 'harp' for us." I couldn't understand it really, but
it was the most beautiful thing someone had ever said to me,
and I experienced joy in my body that was indescribable. Another psychic years later said to me, "I must tell you that I haven't
said this to anyone yet, but you have a blue angel over you. He
is a silent angel of a high rank, and he is there!" I cannot express the deep knowing I felt that this was true, and the lightness I experienced was funny to a point. I felt so light I had
a hard time walking straight afterward. My legs seemed to be
flying, and I felt blessed.

Following those events and a series of others, I bought your
book. One night I was reading your book – the part about human angels – and began to experience much joy and laughter.
My eleven-year-old son woke up to go to the bathroom, and

when he passed in front of my room he asked me what I was laughing about at that time of the night. I answered, "I am reading a book on angels." He took the book and read the part on human angels, and he looked at me and said, "Oh, Mom, we have all those things in the house! Mom, you are an angel!" We laughed and hugged, and he went back to sleep.

Later that night I experienced my "world." I felt an extension of my soul or higher self ascend to a higher realm. It is hard to put this into words, but it was as if I understood (or rather experienced) that time didn't exist, that the body is simply a physical instrument, and felt that "real reality" was in that world above where happiness, lightness, unconditional love, and just being an extension of God was the purpose.

I truly feel that God and his angels are protecting me.

[TLT: Excerpt from a poem Christina wrote:]

Humans are good, and the angels are the mirror of our soul, our first being. May we accept this divinity and let it flow in every cell of our being.

Laurie

San Diego, California

My angel story started in August 1981. My favorite aunt, my godmother, died, and in my grief I examined some old cards she had given me. On one she congratulated me on driving and told me to keep St. Michael by my side. Having been raised as a Catholic and believing in saints and guardian angels, I found this a normal statement. I paid no conscious attention, but for the last five years I have carried a St. Michael medal on my key chain – without knowing why.

I became more curious about Michael and wrote to another aunt, a nun, to ask for details on Michael. She had little literature, but sent my request to a cousin, who mailed me prayer cards and a book on angels. In September I met with a psychic and asked if Michael could be my spirit guide. The answer was yes, but spelled Mikael, the Italian way. Then I read in a book that Mikael is the archangel leading the move through the cosmic door. In some ways I feel complete and absolute knowing that I have a wonderful guide and guardian.

Jacquelyn Heller
Berkeley, California

My real angel story is my life from April 1989 until now. I went to an angel healing group and felt the power of God flow through me in an atmosphere of light and love. I asked for assistance in finding a new place to live. My husband and I were living on Telegraph Avenue in Berkeley in an apartment during a recent riot where people were burning a huge bonfire downstairs from where we lived.

Well, we bought a newspaper for thirty-five cents and found an ad for a place to live in a nearby city. I might note here that I asked for a two-bedroom place, saying I would make one of the rooms an angel room. Well, the place we looked at was too small. Imagine my surprise when the owner of that place called me with news of a couple moving out of a one-bedroom apartment in another building, which is bigger than ours, and suggesting that I give that landlord a call. (How many landlords do you know who would do that?) So we moved in there, two weeks after asking the angels for a place outside of Berkeley. Three months later our next-door neighbor, whom we love, moved out, and we moved into her place, which has two bedrooms.

Things at my job weren't moving, no reclassification, so I turned that over to the angels. Now I work at a large university, where even if one applies for a job, it usually takes three to four months of red tape just to get an interview. I applied for another job at a higher level, and within one week of putting in my application, I got a job interview and was offered the job. That is an angel happening, let me tell you! My whole life has changed. I even make angel porcelain dolls now, and my life and work are filled with the angels. I feel very blessed and receive messages or sense many things from the angels. During our angel healing group, miracles happen to everyone, even long-distance. Our angel healing group includes a world prayer healing at the end of each meeting, so we should see world peace soon and healing for everyone. I would like people to know that they are divine creators with unlimited power.

Diane Munsell

Massachusetts

I was given an angel pin at a weekend retreat by a lovely woman who said, "You are an angel sent from heaven." I thanked her and pinned my guardian angel on my sweater. Later that same day I was driving home and decided to purchase a book for a seminar I was going to be attending the next month. I found the book and pulled it out of the shelf and along with it came *Messengers of Light*—literally falling into my hands!

I thought, "Wow, a book about angels, what a coincidence!" (Or should I say "synchronism.") I took that book and devoured it in two days, bought ANGEL® cards, started my angel conferences and angel mail, and best of all my angel journal. Pulling out of the parking lot that same day, I had a beautiful angel experience. The car parked behind me had a bumper sticker that read, "When in doubt, follow an angel." I laughed and laughed. Then I read about angel experiences, and it all made sense. It is now five months later, and I experience angels all the time. Miracles have happened in my life since I opened up my lines of communication with God and the spiritual world.

Uma Ergil
Tiburon, California

A few days ago I turned on the television and tuned into one depressing story after another. I was overcome with the feeling that our planet is irretrievably lost. I thought, "Angels, we need you! Where are you?" Before the thought was even complete, the screen had burst into a commercial showing several people in a jeep charging across a desert. A voice said something to the effect of "How do you call an angel?" It turned out to be an ad for reruns of the old series "Charlie's Angels." My jaw dropped, and I was instantaneously and delightfully reassured that the angels are right here!

Linda Forster
Carefree, Arizona

I wanted to tell you about my experience during the first week I had your book, *Messengers of Light*. A few unexpected things came up that all but depleted the money I had on hand. My next income was about a week away, so I had a problem. I asked my guardian angel if she would help me out just a little. I figured one hundred dollars would get me through, and things would be fine. I thanked God and my guardian angel for the help I believed I would receive. A couple of days later I bought a lottery ticket just for fun, and then I felt bad, because I thought I was just wasting what little money I had left. Well, the next day I discovered that my lottery ticket had been a winner, and I collected five hundred dollars. What a thrill! I let my friends know how generous my angel had been. What a blessing!!

Clinton Betts
Elizabeth City, North Carolina

It all started in a bookstore in Virginia Beach, Virginia. I saw your book, picked it up, and thumbed through it, then set it back down. I started to walk away, and something hit me. I had the overwhelming urge to go back to the book. I looked through it again and knew I had to have it. There was one problem: I only had enough money to either buy the book or go see a movie I'd been wanting to see for some time. I asked the angels to help me in some way. I went next door and bought a lottery ticket and won ten dollars on the spot. I had enough to get the book, see the movie, and have a wonderful dinner – it turned out quite well!

I finished the book in two days, and while I was taking a shower I thanked my guardian angel for dragging me to the book. In response, I got a rainbow in my bathroom. My most recent encounter came in a meditation. I lay down and stared at the ceiling for a while. Then a figure appeared to be standing beside me. Right away I knew it was my guardian angel. He started waving his hand across my face and out loud I said, "I see you." I felt a smile come from the figure. That night I slept better than I've slept in a long time.

Elsie Madrigal
New Jersey

After reading your book, I saw results instantly when I started talking to my guardian angels and meditating with their help. I have bought at least a dozen guardian angel pins and have given them out and advised others to pray with the aid of their angels. Looking back now, I know I have always been attracted to angels and even named my three sons after the arch-angels: Raphael, Gabriel, and Michael. At the time I named them I did not purposely pick angel names – at least not consciously anyway.

L. Adams
Daytona Beach, Florida

Your book was truly sent to me by an angel. It was even purchased at a store named Angels and Dolphins. When I first started reading your book, I was unfamiliar with the angelic kingdom. The ideas were so foreign to me that I asked for a sign that there were really angels. (My sign: seeing a bird.) The next day I was out taking a walk, and, lo and behold, there was a jolly, kindly gentleman I had never laid eyes on in my neighborhood, and he was walking his dog and carrying a sweet little parrot on his shoulder. When I returned home, I said, "Thank you!"

Now I am beginning to understand why I have been collecting angels like a maniac lately, and also why I have recently purchased a bird. I guess my angels are calling to me!

Your book came into my life at a very low, serious point. I was in therapy and really getting bogged down in seriousness. Since letting angels into my life and asking them for help, *and thanking them for their help,* I am beginning to heal, see the humor in things, laugh more, and generally be more lighthearted. I see a wonderful transformation taking place in myself and my family.

Richard Pineda
Nevada

I am writing to tell you that although I am an inmate at California Men's Colony East, I am very aware of the angels around us. I may call to them under different names and guises, but they are angels from heaven just the same. Since I read your book, *Messengers of Light,* I have been able to more easily sense the presences around me. I am an electronic technician and have become extremely interested in finding and amplifying the vibrational frequencies of the angelic realm. Whether I will be able to achieve this or not, I will continue to meditate and talk to them within. I have found in my searches while I have been incarcerated that the world is a lot different from what I have ever dreamed, but now I can see the beauty and the peace that are and have always been within each of us. Your book has helped me so much in understanding the angelic realm, and although I am not really able to say that I have been in good contact with my guardian angel, I have been able to sense the vibrations around me of goodness, kindness, and love.

I have only seven months left in my sentence, and I would like other prisoners to know that the vibrational patterns of angels can help them as they have helped me.

Visions and Dream-Time Angels

2

We feed our physical bodies with food from the earth. Our minds thrive on knowledge — food for thought. We feed our spirit through dreams, visions, and meditations. The human spirit is free to soar in our imagination. If something exists only in our imagination, does this mean it isn't truth? If something happens to us in our dreams, does this mean we shouldn't be affected by it? If we "see" something only in our mind's eye, does this mean we haven't really seen it? What makes some things fact — truth — and others fiction?

If something can be thought of, dreamed, felt, imagined, visualized, and meditated upon, I say it is as real as you or I. Many "unseen" forces have real effects on us. Just because a field of study called science has not to date been able to measure and prove that angelic forces exist means nothing to me. It is time that we set aside the explanations, forget the experts' statistics, and begin to think and feel for ourselves. We need to become experts on ourselves; then we will truly understand the saying "Know yourself and you will know how to live." The best measure of truth is what you feel in your heart is true. Always keep in mind that "everything is subject to changels!" (Changels are angels of change.)

Visions are important moments in spiritual life. Don't deny yourself visions of angels; look for them and allow them to happen in your life. Keep looking toward the heavens; the angels have many surprises for you. Watch the sky often; the angels use clouds and ice crystal rainbows to create beautiful images that send music and joy to your soul. Go on your own vision quest. No need to do anything to prepare except to be receptive and ask the angels for a glimpse of heaven.

Eileen D.

California

In December I had a most incredible angel dream. It was like a Broadway musical with a group of angels ending the story by singing me a song. The whole meaning of the dream was: *Remember!* Remember your true essence! It was such a beautiful dream; it touched my soul. I woke up with tears of joy in my eyes.

Judith G. Zoch

Chicago, Illinois

Last night I experienced a most incredible dream. A young girl entered my apartment through the wall near the windows. (I live on the twelfth floor of a high-rise building.) I placed a call to my boyfriend, as I couldn't believe what was happening (this was all part of the dream).

I then walked down a hallway in my apartment and requested assistance while the little girl rested. She seemed confused about her situation. I realized she had passed away and was not aware of the transition. As I requested assistance, I was "telepathically" instructed to *trust*. I then fell backward into the arms of what I believe are angels. The angels activated my own wings, and I "knew" what I was supposed to do. I went to the little girl, who was still in a trancelike state. I lifted her into my arms and flew out the window, up through the clouds, where other angels were waiting to receive her.

I feel that I have somehow earned the wings in my earth-bound physicality as a "transitional angel." This may all be part of a vivid imagination via the dream process, but I relate it more to a near-death experience I had in 1989. It was a frightening experience. Without going into detail, I will tell you that I called out for God and all of his angels to save me, and it was at that moment that I believe something of a miracle took place. I was emotionally moved into a state of grace and felt an inner sense of equanimity. I began to vocalize these "feelings" as though singing, but there were no words, only beautiful pitches and tones emanating from within. I felt as though the angels were speaking through me; with every sound, I felt warmth, love, and inspiration.

Tom McClellan

Ontario, Canada

When I was about twenty-three, I had been reading a couple of David Spangler's books and other books by people from Findhorn. I began to feel very frustrated because I knew what they were writing about and felt as if I wasn't accomplishing anything and yet felt I was meant to. I was wondering if I was going to be able to contribute or was going to be looking on the outside as the world changes from a rather childish outlook to one where we are all cocreators with God and the forces around us. With this frustration building up, one night I got down on my knees and prayed. I was crying because I wanted to help so much but felt so isolated.

For the next few days when I meditated I would feel the presence of a very bright being as I visualized my "meeting room" in the special meditation I used, along with the saints and people I admired. I was afraid to see who this being was because he seemed so powerful. After ducking out of a confrontation with this being for a few days, I was dreaming and had a vision. I was taken above the earth, and this great being of a golden vibration—it was like golden sparkles filling the blackness of space—surrounded me and enveloped me. Then I felt my own vibrations raising as they blended with his. As this was happening, I was telepathically asking, "Who are you?" and was answered or felt myself saying, *"Our Father who art in Interplanetary Brotherhood."*

When I start to feel down at times, I sometimes think of this being and find peace. One time when I was really going through some hard personal interactions and was fighting back the urge to be depressed or feel sorry for myself or be aggressive and I said, "No! I am going to be joyful in spite of all this," I could feel this being say, "You have chosen well." I feel good sharing these memories with you for they help me again in recounting them. Now when I think of him, he is always laughing.

Dorothy Rials

Brookhaven, Massachusetts

I am a widow of sixty-four. I am very spiritual; all I have in this world is God, the holy spirit, angels, and the saints.

Whenever I have a crisis in my family, I ask God to tell me what it is all about, and he does through dreams. My daughter was found to have cancer and it had spread, so I asked God for help. For five nights in a row I went through asking about the breast, how the cancer had spread to the bones, and so forth. The last night in my dreams there were five cherubim close together above my bed. I woke up happy, reaching for an angel. They had come to comfort me. The next day I asked God to stop because I was exhausted. I might forget a trivial dream, but never a revelation from God.

Jessie Nelson
Mound, Minnesota

I was going through a stressful time in my life (a divorce). I am a flight attendant and was on a layover in Houston. I went to my room after a long day. I got ready for bed and lay down on the bed. I felt someone lie down next to me. I jumped up, but no one was there. I then looked through my room, again making sure my doors were locked, and so forth. I lay back down, and again I felt as if someone had nudged me or bumped my hip; this time it felt playful. I then heard tinkling glass coming from a distance—a very peaceful sound. The next thing I heard was beautiful laughter, which made me laugh. I went into a half-awake, half-asleep state, and in this state I saw thousands of small sparkles of many colors twinkling. I tried to make all of this sound logical in my mind, but I gave up. I chose to believe that my room that night in Houston was full of angels. I feel

31

gifted to have had this experience and since then have had a few more similar experiences.

Elon Carina Makala
Washington

Until I read your book, I hadn't thought of asking the angels to help in the many ways that you suggested. Now I connect with them many times a day. One day I was channeling some energy to assist a friend, and the thought came to me that it would be nice to have some angels with us. So I asked for a roomful of angels. Ah, be careful what you wish for! The room was suddenly so crowded with angels that I could "hear" wings rustling and feel a couple of wings brush the side of me and the top of my head. After a good laugh, I suggested maybe a few angels would be enough.

One of the most amazing, and at that time unexpected, experiences I have had with angels happened at the end of a memorial service for one of my husband's cousins. I spent the entire service in a meditative state without a preconceived idea of what would happen. It was very beautiful. As the minister was finishing his remarks, I felt the ceiling of the circular chapel lift off and open to the heavens. Then I saw a circle of angels gather around with others in the middle of their circle. As people began to file out of the chapel, I heard (it was more like experienced) the angels singing. I've seldom felt as close to heaven as I did at that moment. Truly, together we are all one!

Martha H. Rush

Texas

Expected Miracle

Great preparations had been made for the Feast of the Assumption at St. John Neuman's Catholic Church in Lubbock, Texas. It was a very hot evening on August 15, 1988, and more than thirteen thousand people had gathered for an expected miracle. At 6:15 P.M. the event was being televised before an outdoor altar that had been prepared the previous week or so. However, I was in my apartment several miles from the church. Suddenly, the anxious announcer said, "I don't know what's happening, but everyone is facing the west looking toward the sun."

I ran upstairs and looked out the window. I first saw the sun's rays—very brilliant and impossible to look at for very long. I watched the clouds when Mary appeared in profile, wearing robes, a flowing scarf, and what seemed to be a wreath in her hair. She was facing a cherub, and when she kissed the cherub it disappeared. The clouds were not the kind you can imagine looking like an elephant or bird; the face seemed to emerge from the clouds.

Then there was a man's face; he exuded power, and light from within shone from his eyebrows, eyes, and all around his face. He looked quite stern but not frightening. I was stunned when a huge rose-colored cloud surrounded him as he disappeared.

Mary turned full face toward me, very sweet and serene. Another smaller cloud, a darker shade of rose, engulfed her, and she, too, disappeared. You must realize these clouds were not a sunset color at all—it was much too early for sunset at

6:15 anyway. I had never seen colors such as these in the sky at any time. It was reported the next day that many others had seen Mary, Jesus, and those beautiful rose clouds.

The whole episode didn't last long, probably five to ten minutes, but it was truly wonderful—a miracle I'll never forget.

[TLT: The reason Martha titled this "Expected Miracle" is because, starting in 1988, each year on August 15 people meet to seek a sign—or miracle—from God.]

Terra Frank
Hawaii

I have mentally seen my personal angel. He surrounded me in a gold light and wrapped me in his beautiful wings, which looked like a large white cloak. The gold light entered the top of my head and then flowed through my body. I do not know his name yet. He is so magnificent. Little angels come to me also. They dance around me and shower me with their dazzling dust of light and flowers.

Rita K. Fecek
Ohio

As I told you in the past, Father Maguire told me my angel's name was "Jill." Well, I went to a seminar entitled "Meeting Your Guardian Angel," and it was awesome. The seminar ended with a meditation led by Michael Pearl, which concluded with meeting our guardian angels. By creative visualization, fabulous music, and a wonderful man leading us, I met and saw Jill (again). She was beautiful–robed in a white gown with a golden chord around her waist and beautiful large wings. Jill embraced me, and I cried. She told me she was glad that I was telling people about their guardian angels and that because it has brought her so much happiness she was changing her name to Joy. She told me to remind people that their angels are always with them. They are always here; you don't have to call them down from the heavens.

People had so many different experiences that we shared with each other. It was beautiful. One man asked his angel why he hadn't talked to or seen him before, and the angel told him, "You weren't listening!" We were told that angels have no conception of time, so we should take that into consideration with our requests. Also, they do not speak to us verbally. They talk to us through our subconscious–or put the thoughts into our heads. There's so much I am finding out, and I am still collecting angels, figurines, and so forth, and I'm finding so many different ones. Now all I need is money to buy them!

C. A. Jung
New York

I saw my first angel while meditating at an angel gathering. First I saw a miniature female angel with a crowbar. She was trying to pry my heart open, but couldn't. Then another one came, and then another–they did it. I always thought I had an open heart; maybe being in New York makes it close down without my awareness. Funny image, isn't it?

Extraordinary Visitations
and Communications

3

Ask a roomful of people what their favorite movie is, and I would bet at least one person would answer, "It's a Wonderful Life." The movie begins in heaven as we hear prayers offered up for George Bailey, the main character in the story. Then we listen to God and St. Joseph discuss who will be sent to earth for George's benefit. Many of us pray every day. Prayer is usually something people do in private. The reason I know people pray is not because they have told me; it is just something I know in my heart. Prayer is a way to communicate with the angels, and they are the answers to our prayers; they are God's emissaries sent to us and others by request. Sometimes we may make our own request consciously or unconsciously, or someone else will on our behalf. Many amazing things happen through the intercession of prayer. To the many people praying, I say, "Keep it up! God listens!"

It's a Wonderful Life is a movie about angel help at its finest. Clarence is an angel who has yet to earn his wings. God decides to give Clarence his chance, and he is sent to earth to rescue George Bailey in his darkest hour. Clarence tells George, after hearing a bell ring on a cash register, "Every time a bell rings, an angel gets its wings." Bells are ringing all over the place. I hear them in these letters and when people share their angel experiences with me. Many angels are getting their wings as they help us humans cope with a changing, fast-paced world.

Angels are messengers who can arrange things so that we are saved from imminent danger. They leave wonderful scents that give us a sense of peace, calm, and hope. Many angel experiences involve light. Angels can appear as light to remind us to "enlighten up." Angels *have been thought to appear as humans at crucial times when help is needed. In this section, letter writers share experiences of visits from angels who were called in either consciously by prayer, or unconsciously by guardian angel telepathy. The angels are always near.*

Terry Lynn Taylor

Years ago I went on a camping trip with some friends to an island belonging to a Marine base near Cherry Point, South Carolina. My friend's brother was an officer at this base and gave us a ride by boat out to the island and dropped us off with enough supplies for a couple of days. This was not a designated campground; it was incredibly beautiful, and we were the only humans on this island. One afternoon I decided to take a walk by myself into the woods. I was walking along without a care in the world when suddenly my body froze in a position with my right foot in the air, about to step down. Even my breathing stopped for a moment. I looked down at the path before me, and right where my foot would have come down was a very large rattlesnake crossing my path. The snake didn't even notice me, and I watched it gracefully make its way into the grass and disappear. Then my body unfroze, and I knew immediately that my guardian angel had stopped me from stepping on the snake, which would most likely have caused it to snap its head back and bite my leg in self-defense. That would have been quite a predicament because we were on a secluded island without any way to get off until someone came to get us. I thanked God for the intervention and continued my walk. As I walked along, a negative and fearful scenario played over in my mind of what could have happened. I soon realized that this was counterproductive and that I should be joyous over the direct example that I had received of angels watching over me. With this realization, I felt a state of grace come upon me, and I knew that everything would ultimately be okay!

Jeanne
California

Dedicated to Maureen, with love

My sister Maureen was a stillbirth, and I never knew her on the physical plane. But as the years have passed I know she has never left my side. There are times I feel her very strongly, and I know deep in my heart she has to be one of my guardian angels. So I dedicate my letter to her, for the unconditional love and support she has transmitted to me.

I recently have had two visitations by angels, and it definitely has made a positive change in my life. I was so unhappy in the last year; my life was full of sickness. I had two surgeries six months apart, and all I did was sit around being depressed and sad. My husband at this point didn't know what to do.

My in-laws have a house in the mountains, and we decided to get away with the kids. I thought this might help, but I only felt worse. The second night of our stay, my daughter, who is seventeen months old, was sleeping in our room. She woke up, and I took care of her needs, then put her to sleep again. I went back to bed but could not get back to sleep. I tossed and turned for a while, when suddenly, as I was lying on my back, I noticed an angel at the top of the ceiling. A small beautiful angel in white, holding its hand out to me. I said to myself, I must be dreaming. I decided to hold my hand out to the angel, and an incredible force drew me up to it. As we connected and touched hands, I knew it wasn't a dream. I have never felt such utter peace and happiness. It was as if it was telling me everything was going to be okay. I remember afterward, lying back in my bed, looking around and thinking how incredible this all was as my husband and daughter lay there sleeping. I smelled the distinct scent of sandalwood for a moment, and then it was gone.

The second occurrence happened at dusk. I was sitting quietly on my bed looking out the window. I realized I wasn't alone; I had six angels, cute little cherubim, dancing around me as if they were engaged in some kind of party. They were so happy and playful! This went on for about five minutes, and then they were gone as fast as they had come. In the corner of my room I felt a strong presence, a glorious angel, so tall it stood from the floor to the ceiling adorned in white and gold, standing directly in front of me. Its vibrations were so strong that as I stood there I felt my feet lift off the ground a few times as if I could fly, but each time this happened I would fall down. Then it disappeared, but I still felt a strong presence in the room that lasted for about an hour afterward.

To say the least, my life has not been the same since. I have not told many people of my experiences because I feel they wouldn't understand. Your book prompted me to write to you. I truly believe in angels and believe they are here to help us and guide us.

Cheri Leslie

Fourth Dimension Bookstore, Venice, California

I have realized that angels have guided my life long before I was fully aware of their interaction in my daily activities. As a child I played with fairies and little people until my parents convinced me it was my imagination, so I forgot them as I grew older. I was raised with the belief that I had a guardian angel, but until I was an adult I didn't know my guardian angel was an unseen presence that truly guided and protected me. In my midtwenties, with small children, my marriage was a shambles. I was depressed, and my life was chaotic. Late one night, feeling alone and desperate, I contemplated suicide. With a kitchen knife before me, I laid my head on the table and collapsed in tears, crying to God for help. There was an immediate presence that enveloped me, lifting me from my chair. Holding and supporting my body, this presence led me to the drawer to put the knife away and then up the stairs to bed.

Years later, as a single parent living in California, I became aware of angels as a real and present help in times of trouble. Leaving my house one morning, I stumbled and fell forward. There are over a dozen concrete steps leading up to the house. I mentally claimed there were no accidents. A power caught me by the shoulders, and I felt myself being turned in midair to an upright position, and then I was placed on a concrete step. I sat thanking the angels for this intervention as my dogs licked my face. I went inside to put on different panty hose since the pair I was wearing had gotten ripped. I was not shaken up in the least but very calm, as if the event had never occurred.

One evening while reading, I suddenly saw the front of a semi-trailer truck, all bright chrome and headlights. I felt the truck crushing my chest and heard one of my children calling, "Mom!" I pushed the truck away with force and began to affirm that God was present, and there were no accidents. I mentally envisioned a white light around my daughter, who had earlier taken the car out to go to the store. I didn't look at the clock because I did not want to give in to the thought of mortal time, but affirmed that we are always eternal and spiritual. I prayed for a long time, until I felt a sense of peace. When my daughter arrived home, I gave thanks for the protection. The next day my son called me from Berkeley, where he'd gone to visit a friend, to tell me he would not be driving home that night but would leave first thing the following morning. I asked why he had changed his plans, and he said he was tired and while driving to Berkeley he had fallen asleep at the wheel of his car, waking up just in time to avoid a collision with a semi-trailer truck, as his car drifted into oncoming traffic.

I awoke once in the middle of the night to find a visible white light active and moving on the dresser to the right of my bed. It was neither large nor small, but I knew instantly it was my angel. As I got out of bed, I said hello as naturally as could be and went into the bedroom. When I returned, the light was gone, but I knew my angel was definitely in the room.

Recently at a street festival held where my business was located, one of the gals who worked for me mentioned that sales were very slow compared to the previous day. I sat outside the store watching the people stroll by and called upon the angels.

I affirmed that everything was in harmony, that people were having a good time, and that there was prosperity. I affirmed that my store (a metaphysical book and gift store) offered items to support people in realizing their highest level of consciousness. I could see and feel an angelic white light above the store entrance. As I continued to affirm the universal truths about harmony and prosperity, people began walking in the door. Within minutes, the store was filled with people and more continued to come in until I told the angels thank-you—that it was enough.

Kathleen Ann Milner
Wisconsin

During my workshop on angelic light, I was asked by Spirit to work with seven archangels and the seven rays. Their presence and power were experienced throughout the workshop in many ways. It was toward the end of the session when one of the archangels sent a blast of white light into the room. All the participants who had their eyes open at that moment saw it. The gentleman who was my volunteer went out to see if there had been a power surge in the building, and there hadn't been. The light came from a point of origin on the wall where there was no light fixture or electrical outlet of any kind. My feeling is that the light carried with it something for everyone who was present. I was also told by Spirit that the angels will continue to make visible other realities from different dimensions at group gatherings.

Hal Schwettman
Ohio

Here are a few comments about my angels. I remember that about the time I started to meditate and read about spiritual things I started to see white flashes of light on the wall. I had never seen these before, and I thought it was my physical eyes. I found out later that I was seeing the energy of my guides when they came around me. When I tune in for meditation or when I'm channeling healing energy, I can sometimes see the flashes of light, mostly with my eyes closed.

In your book, you mentioned that angels love candles. I have found this to be very true. When my wife and I connect with God to channel his healing energy, we light one white candle. I remember when we first did this I was doing a healing on my wife, and I got the thought to look at the candle. When I did, the flame was extremely high on the candle. A normal candle flame is about an inch and a half high. When our guides and healing angels are near, the flame is around three inches or more high. I know that whenever you connect with God and are in tune with the Christ Light for healing, your guides and healing angels come. They are attracted by that, and they love to be a part of the healings. I have a healing angel who works with me when I do healings. This angel is a doctor in spirit. In a past-life reading, I was given his name and told he was my healing teacher in a past life. It took me some years to learn how he works with me. He guides me through thoughts and feelings about where to put my hands. I can feel the healing light vary in intensity through my hands. He will also come in at times when I'm not expecting it, and my finger will get hot from the healing energy. At those times there may be someone near who needs a healing. I remember one lady whom I did a healing on who could see my guide out of the corner of her eye. She saw him giving me instructions for the healing.

Patricia Walton
Paoli, Pennsylvania

It was the first time we were at Disneyworld after awakening to the existence of our family of angels and guides, and we really went there as a group this time. When we checked into the Contemporary Hotel, the room we had requested on the Magic Kingdom side was unavailable, and we were given a poolside room for the first night. The next morning—my husband's fiftieth birthday—he looked sleepily out of the window to see the beach cleaner had written in the sand a huge "I ♥ YOU" directly below our window. Whether or not that was customary, Disney magic didn't matter, because we are sure it was our angel friends who arranged the room change for one night just so he could be surprised with the early morning greeting of affection.

Our twenty-seventh anniversary shortly followed Ray's birthday, and unfortunately that morning we had an argument that ended in tears and hurt feelings. After we calmed down, we turned to our guides, and they soothed us and calmly guided us to fill the room with, and then breathe in, first pink, then green, then white light. We followed their instructions, and soon all was well again, and we prepared to leave our room. As we opened the door, we found a beautiful flower arrangement sitting on the floor beside our door. No one we knew had sent it, and the guests in the room on each side of us said it was not theirs. We checked with the hotel desk to see if it was meant for another floor, and then with the Disneyworld flower shop to see if they knew of it. They were adamant that it could not possibly have been delivered to us without a card of some sort, without any identification.

Perplexed, we turned to our angel friends to ask if they knew anything about the flowers. They asked us what color the flowers were. The entire arrangement was done in three colors: pink, green, and white. Then they asked us to count the blooms in the arrangement. There were twenty-one—exactly the number of our combined family of angels, guides, and teachers at that time. Then they wished us happy anniversary and suggested we all get ourselves over to the Magic Kingdom and have some fun!

On the last day we were there, we were told that a new angel guide had been added to my husband's "team"—one who presents herself as a young woman named Christine. Shortly after he began sunbathing that day, on the hotel's beach, he felt a drop of water drip onto his midriff. He opened his eyes and raised his head to see if anyone was near, or if there was perspiration there. His skin was still dry, and no water or person was nearby. He clearly felt this, and we were later told that it was a tear of joy Christine shed when she began her first "shift" as his guide. She promised to prove that he hadn't imagined it by doing something else to surprise us before we left. We wondered if we had misunderstood, because it was our last night there and we were leaving early the next day to catch our plane. About 4:00 A.M. I awakened, sat up, and looked at the sliding glass doors leading to our twelfth-floor balcony – inaccessible to any other. The windows fogged over each night because of the air conditioning inside. They had also fogged over this night, with the exception of a huge backward "C" written on the outside of the glass that extended from nearly the top to the bottom of the glass door. The width was about a foot wide and looked as if it had just been drawn by someone standing outside on our balcony, which couldn't have been anyone except an angel named Christine who was determined to keep her promise.

We traveled home on an airplane from that trip, but I really think we could have flown home without it! We felt so loved, and so spoiled. I kept asking the angels why they went to so much trouble, and they simply said it was fun to make us so happy!

Joanna Schohl
Wisconsin

I am fascinated by the focus of your work – "angel consciousness" and perception of life. This has certainly been an evolving piece of my journey in the past few years. Often now I automatically appeal to the angels for blessing, protection, or guidance. The reality of their intimate participation in our lives is very clear to me. I continue to have "moments" of realization or recognition of their presence. One night, not too long ago, I woke up and found myself half asleep, trying to pull up my blanket, as I had gotten cold in the night. I had a very clear image of a "mother" angel bending over me and covering me up with a gentle, nurturing hand. Another night, I woke up to go to the bathroom about 3:00 A.M. and upon returning smelled a lovely sweet floral fragrance surrounding my bed. The aroma was distinctively beautiful. I went back to sleep calmly and easily.

Donna M. Freeman
Colorado

This is one of three angel experiences I had during my husband's sixteen-month hospital stay, all of which could have been disastrous if not for the protection of my angel—this I truly believe.

It was in the early fall of 1949. My husband was in the hospital in Van Nuys, California, which was approximately sixty miles from our home in the East Los Angeles area. One Sunday evening while I was visiting him, he asked if I would mind taking another patient's girlfriend into Hollywood as she had no way home. I had only been driving about a year and was rather apprehensive about doing this, but I agreed as there was no bus service that ran late near the hospital—it being somewhat out in the "toolies" at that time.

As we departed the exit gate at 10:00 P.M., I found I had no brakes on our 1937 Chevrolet coupe. I thought, Now what do I do? No money, late at night, nothing around, and I have to get to Hollywood and then home. The only thing I could do was put my faith in God and ask my guardian angel for help. To make a long story short, I did make it to Hollywood (a great distance out of my way) and then home—ending up very nervous and exhausted! The next day my brother-in-law told me

I had no master cylinder, and he didn't know how I, a novice driver, had made that drive. But I knew—my angel had heeded my prayer, and if he hadn't been my copilot I shudder to think of what serious accident could have occurred. I felt his presence there in the seat beside me, particularly from Hollywood to home that one late Sunday night that I'll never forget.

Pauline Gough
Washington

[TLT: Pauline facilitates an angel group whose members meet and share stories.]

In January 1987 I flew to Los Angeles with a stop in Oakland en route. On the return trip as we were approaching the Oakland airport, I became aware of the aura of the airplane and realized we were being held there in the light. I was flooded with a feeling of immense joy. This is a wonderful memory, and this experience made the greatest impression. I have noticed many people have angel experiences as children or teenagers and then again in their forties.

At age seventeen, with my boyfriend (who is now my husband of thirty-three years) and a girlfriend, the car I was driving spun out of control on black ice. My girlfriend was thrown into a snowbank on the side of the road, and Brian and I came right to the brink of a ravine, where the car stopped. We were all okay. Dorothy Fischer, a very special angel to all who know her and a member of our angel group, agreed to share a similar experience for your book.

Dorothy Fischer
Washington

It was late summer or early fall, and we were having a glorious "Indian summer." My daughter Christy, aged ten, and I were making a move to the Grand Canyon from Vancouver, Washington.

The trip was going well, and we had gone as far as Marry's Hill Pass by late evening. It was still light and sunny when we topped the hill. Then suddenly we went from clear highway to snow and black ice. The car did a complete circle and was headed for the edge of the cliff. I was helpless. There was nothing to stop us. I saw the edge coming up and yelled, "Stop," and the car simply stopped. Just in time—no inches to spare.

Christy and I sat in *thanksgiving,* with tears streaming down our faces. Finally I collected my wits, backed up, drove back onto the highway, and continued our trip. As we reached the bottom of the pass, we saw a little motel and a truck stop. We were so spent from the near-death event that we decided to spend the night (regardless of the smell and dinginess). We were just *thankful* for a place to stop and rest. When morning arrived, we looked out to discover it had snowed heavily, and the wind had blown big drifts of snow everywhere. Most of the road had disappeared. We decided to join three truck drivers having breakfast. They were waiting to see if the sun would melt some of the snow and the wind would settle. About 10:00 A.M. we followed the trucks out of the storm area.

Had there been no motel, or truck stop, and nothing to do but travel on, we would surely have been lost—possibly stranded and perhaps frozen to death. Christy and I felt we had experienced a double miracle! Isn't that what life is? Thank you for our guardian angel, dear God!

Dagmar Maria Mack
Pasadena, California

I have for a long time believed that we are surrounded and guided by angelic beings. About fifteen years ago, Erick, my husband, our young children, and I were in a terrible snow blizzard coming down a mountain road from the Big Bear area. There was no visibility at all. All of a sudden we felt like something pushed our station wagon back. When Erick got out of the car, he found we were two feet away from a two hundred–foot cliff. It was very frightening to think that we were so close to death, yet I felt a warmth and knew we were protected.

Penny Popiel
Winnipeg, Manitoba, Canada

You must be included as one of the angels in my life called "Terry" whom I beckoned into my life a couple of years ago. You are late in arriving. I have sent you a copy of my story of an angel situation I wrote before I ever heard of ANGEL® cards or your great book.

Miracle of Faith

A few years ago, one day in August, I was home from work and feeling depressed. I had a biopsy on my ankle and was waiting for it to mend and for the results from the specialist.

I had been estranged from my two children for three years because my ex-husband had turned them against me in bitterness after I divorced him. I was thinking of my children, especially with Christmas only four months away. How was I going to handle missing them so?

I had prayed to God for support many times before, but this day I thought that maybe he was too busy for my prayers, and I decided to call from above my sister Terry Martin, who had committed suicide about eight years earlier. In my prayer, I said, "Dear Terry, you must have earned your wings by this time. Please send me strength and a sign to help me face my ordeals with my leg and my children." I was feeling very upset that day and very alone. I cried myself to sleep. About an hour later, I was awakened by the doorbell. Two ladies in their twenties were at my front door. They introduced themselves as missionaries from the Mormon Church. I was just about to bid them farewell when I noticed that one lady had a name pin on her lapel that said "Sister Terry."

I invited them in for tea, and the rest is history. Sister Susan Terry said that they were just strolling by and decided to try to do some angel work with their mission. I told them about my prayers to my sister, Terry Martin. They became my friends and returned many times to pray with me.

My leg healed perfectly, and my son came home at Christmas and has remained close to me. Most of my prayers were answered. Thank God and thank Sister Terry.

Gina Q.

Arizona

For two years my grandmother had been very ill and close to death on numerous occasions; however, this was a woman who did *not* want to die! She defied all! Well, this spring she declined very rapidly and began having a lot of pain. On April 7, I awoke about 5:00 A.M. with her on my mind. I lay there and I had a conversation with her in my mind that went like this: "Nana, don't be afraid. You have so many beautiful angels waiting to guide you and be with you. They will help you! Nana, our faith teaches us that you are going to be with God, so reach out to the angels and don't be afraid." Then I asked my angels to race to her and give her courage. My Nana died at 5:15 A.M.

Linda H.

Pasadena, California

August 10, 1992

One year ago my adopted brother and friend, Randy, died of AIDS. I was in daily contact with him for the last six months of his life here. It was a time of varied emotional intensities, ranging from sadness and frustration to deep compassion.

Randy was nineteen when he learned he had AIDS, and he lived until he was twenty-nine. He fought his disease and rarely revealed the level of physical pain he endured. He maintained a sharp awareness, wit, and interest in life.

When we spent time together there was an unspoken commitment to enjoy every moment. The simplest pleasures we identified, devoured, and savored. I learned to slow down with Randy. Together we delighted in the flavors of fine food, the fragrance of April roses, and the feel of differently textured fabrics. We shared an appreciation for the mood-altering effects of various shades of the color blue. We had a lot of silly fits of laughter as well.

Two months before Randy's passing, we took a slow stroll on a warm summer evening with the intention of doing some stargazing. We wandered down the lengthy driveway alongside his apartment building. He was in too much pain to walk quickly or often, but he always made the effort. As we traveled, we became aware of a cool breeze. We described its effect on the surrounding treetops and bushes, and how soft and soothing it felt on our skin. We inhaled the scented summer blend of sweet gardenias and recently watered lawns. As we moved, the breeze developed a new strength. We laughed and lifted our welcoming arms. Time seemed to slow down. I imagined the wind was receiving us as well.

We reached the end of the driveway, turned, and sat on the steps in front of the apartment building. The breeze followed us there, continuing to stir our clothes, twisting and cooling our hair. We giggled. We spoke softly to one another. A dreamy quality engulfed us. I don't recall the conversation, but I felt a peaceful, loving exchange floating between us and around us. I *knew* an angel was present. The sensation remained after we went inside and for days afterward. We often shared the memory of that special evening.

Randy was aware of the presence of his guardian angel

when he was young. He believed she had abandoned him during his illness. I asked my friend Terry about absent angels, and she told me the story called "Footprints" and related it to angels. I later relayed the story to Randy.

Not long after our windy summer evening experience, Randy joyfully told me he knew his guardian angel had returned. I now believe she revealed herself to us that night. I also realize her wings blessed us with a lovely breeze, and her presence filled us with peace.

Windy summer nights now have a new and special meaning for me. They not only remind me of longing and loss, but bring me confidence that angels present themselves through nature. Perhaps the wind is often an angel traveling nearby to comfort, soothe, tickle, and reassure us, to restore faith and bring us blessings through breezes.

Terry Lynn Taylor

For those of you who haven't yet heard the story Linda H. mentioned in her letter, I offer one version here. The author is unknown.

Footprints.

One night a man had a dream. He dreamed he was walking along the beach with the Lord. Across the sky flashed scenes from his life. For many scenes, he noticed two sets of footprints in the sand—one belonging to him and the other to the Lord.

When the last scene of his life flashed before him, he looked back at the footprints in the sand. He noticed that many times along the path of his life there was only one set of footprints. He also noticed that this was the case at the very lowest and saddest times in his life.

This really bothered him, and he questioned the Lord about it. "Lord, you said that once I decided to follow you, you'd walk with me all the way. But I have noticed that during the most troublesome times in my life, there is only one set of footprints. I don't understand why when I needed you most, you would leave me."

The Lord replied, "My precious, precious child, I love you, and I would never leave you. During your times of trial and suffering, when you see only one set of footprints, it was then that I carried you."

Flo Llamzon
California

Your book came to me at a time in my life when I really, really needed a lift. I was taking life much too seriously; and it showed. As a side note, I had gotten up early this morning and was standing at the kitchen sink fixing my dog's breakfast when I felt a gentle breeze on my face and looked up to see if my fern hanging overhead was being gently blown from the same breeze; it was not. There was no physical explanation for this—no window or door was open. The event lasted about fifteen seconds. It stopped as suddenly as it had begun. It was such a magical moment for me, because I realized my guardian angel was very near and letting me know it was okay to believe.

Alice McKinney
Minnesota

On the night of June 19, 1974, I was on my way to my mother's house because my stepfather, whom I loved very much, had just died. I remarked to the friend who was with me, "Do you notice the overwhelming scent of jasmine in the car?" She didn't, but I sure did. All the way to my mother's house, I noticed the scent. I felt at the time that it was my stepfather's way of letting me know he was all right.

B. A. Kuczynski
Linden, New Jersey

One Saturday morning a few coworkers and I were putting in some overtime in Linden Municipal Court. I was sitting toward the back of the office inputting information from old traffic tickets, when my friend Carol turned to me from the front of the office and said, "I smell roses." Bess, my youngest daughter, had stopped by and was with Carol in the front helping her file tickets. Bess looked at Carol and shook her head because she knew what was coming. "No, really," Carol insisted, "don't you smell roses?" Bess asked her, "Does my mother drive all of you nuts with her angel stories? She does us at home." Carol told her that I hadn't mentioned angels at all. (She obviously hadn't been listening to me.) I told her that smelling the roses meant that her angel was trying to get her attention, and a discussion ensued. Carol kind of "okeydokeyed" me and we both went back to our work. When I looked down at the next ticket on my pile, I said (a few times), "Oh my God." Bess, concerned that something had happened, came rushing back to see if I was okay. The first name of the person on the very next ticket was (what else?) Angel. Carol said she will get a copy of your book and doesn't okeydokey me anymore!

Renaté Maria Bell
Lake Mary, Florida

After reading your suggestion about asking for your angel's name, I verbally requested my guardian's name before going to bed the same evening. The following morning, a Thursday, I reminded myself as I drove to work to have my car battery looked at that coming weekend. The oldies' song "Johnny Angel" came on while I was at work. I had to smile. When I left work Thursday evening, the car wouldn't start—not a sound. After jump-starting it and keeping the battery in contact with pliers, I drove nervously down the highway to the service station. The entire stretch I kept saying out loud, "Be with me; get me there." I got there, and walked to a nearby bookstore, which I normally frequent while waiting for the car to be serviced. This time, however, I decided to go down a different aisle. I didn't know why I had chosen this aisle because I had to backtrack, but when I walked into the aisle, centered eye level on the middle shelf in bold red letters, was *Angels*, a large hard-covered book. I instinctively knew I had help and protection while driving my car. As I arrived home, with a new battery, I put the stereo on. I thanked the angels out loud for getting me home safe. I was happy, and now my weekend was free. Not three minutes later, "Johnny Angel" came on the radio again. Now, if I need cheering up, guidance, or protection, I automatically sing, "Johnny Angel, you're an angel to me. . . . "

Urithrael
Florida

Your book has the same atmospheric angels that I know. By that I mean the lightness and lack of somberness that is usually found in descriptions of angels. We are blessed with at least two types of angelic beings you might be interested in. The most spectacular one appeared above the coffin of a dear friend during a perfectly terrible "religious" church ceremony. The angel appeared "in majesty," with gorgeous robes of light, and was about twelve feet tall. The sense I received was of unbelievable power, tempered with a calm joy and completeness. That might sound strange, but that's the way it felt.

Another type that appears more regularly is also very tall and columnar with fairly rigid floor-length bronze-green garments. The sense I have of them is utterly silent and watchful. These beings appear in our offices, at home, and in a few other special locales. They appear in pairs, forming what feels like a gateway. They will stand around the perimeter of our round office reception area to meditate there and will appear singularly for no apparent reason.

The angels helped us relocate to another city and buy our house. With very little money, we were trying to move closer to our business, thinking that we would have to rent something again. Even so, we were looking at a house for sale with a beautiful lot full of trees all overgrown and neglected, with the idea of creative financing. My husband asked me if I had any "feeling" about the place, and I said, facetiously, that I would feel better about trying for the house if I could see an angel on the roof. We left the house and I told my husband, "It sounds weird, but since I said that about the angel on the roof, I do 'see' an angel on the roof." That was all he needed to hear. He made an offer, with no money down, full of 11-11s, and it was accepted! The address is 1122, and not only is the primary angel still on the roof, but often we sense smaller versions under the eaves. The grounds are full of devas and other beings, and we are just beginning to open to their intelligences to cocreate a magical environment. Our desire is to create a house of light for other angels, human and otherwise, to visit.

P.S. Our angels do not have wings, and the primary house angel always appears to be wearing gold lamé!

Barb Martin

Wisconsin

I have always had a guardian angel, but I'm afraid that I have forgotten it often and allowed many fears and anxieties to cloud my days. My husband, Rick, and I have long joked about his role as my guardian angel. A psychic once told me that he only returned "this time" to be with me and to act in that role. He is truly an angel—most of the time.

I know that my mother received specific help from two angels some years ago. She had accompanied me on a business trip to San Francisco. She elected to take part in a bus tour, but upon arrival at the tour's destination found that she really didn't like the park and wanted to leave. The return bus was not due to arrive for approximately five hours. She started to walk, thinking she would catch a city bus, although she was a long way from San Francisco. She was walking along Highway 101! No, she's not crazy—just a bit eccentric. She was walking along, to where?—none of us are certain—when from nowhere a boy on a bicycle appeared and said, "Lady, where are you going?" At this point, she noticed that she was about to walk onto the freeway. Somehow she made it to a bus stop. While waiting for a bus, a group of three "none-too-friendly-looking" males started to approach her, and she was afraid. Then, suddenly, a man came walking up, whistling, and at his appearance, the group disappeared. The man, who spoke in a heavy British accent, then accompanied her on the bus, all the way into San Francisco to our hotel. She doesn't even remember his name. If not an angel, certainly he was a messenger from heaven.

K. Martin-Kuri

Waquoit, Massachusetts

I awakened one morning and turned to my night table to put my single contact lens into my one good eye. To my dismay, the lens was not in the container. Apparently, in my exhaustion the night before, I had been unaware that the lens had stayed on my finger and not been placed in the storage cap. I realized that the lens, which was of the hard variety, had obviously become lost in bedding, or was on the carpet. In a panic, I put on my regular glasss, but I could not see well, as many lens wearers will attest to if they use the lenses 100 percent of the time. Despite the blur, I looked, and looked, and there was no lens to be found anywhere.

This particular morning was unusually important to me. I was to meet with the representative of the resort where the American Conference on Angels was being held in May 1992. It was vital that I attend since I was the designer of the event. I would not be able to drive with the eyeglasses, and I did not have a spare lens. Unfortunately, I had postponed getting a spare for many months. With all these concerns, I felt truly desperate. I knelt down and pleaded with my guardian angel. I said that if the angels wanted to hold the conference, and I was to attend this vital meeting, I would need their help in locating the lens. I focused on all the love and care that the angels had for my work. I became inwardly very still. Then I heard a gentle whisper to go into the bathroom a few feet away. I thought, how strange, surely the lens was not in there! But I trusted that angelic whisper and crawled on my knees into the bathroom. I remember thinking, Well, anything is possible; maybe the lens bounced really far. However, there was no lens to be found anywhere on the bathroom floor. I kept calm. Then I heard another gentle whisper, almost like a caress, telling me to turn around and head back into the bedroom. As I did this and looked ahead, I saw a shiny spot on the carpet. There it was! Tears welled up within me as I realized how my angel had positioned me to find the lens, which I couldn't possibly have seen before from the direction in which I had been.

The message was quite powerful, and I would like to share it. So many times in our lives we can't seem to find something we know is critical to our work, to our very survival. And we keep hopelessly wandering about, looking everywhere without success. But if we trust and seek the help of God, through his servers that love and protect us, we can do the seemingly impossible. What is so interesting is that if we follow divine guidance while in a state of quiet trusting, we may be led to take actions that seem on the surface unproductive, or seem to go in the opposite direction. But such a repositioning might be all that is necessary. I think that our angels often want us to see things from a new viewpoint, a fresh perspective that will lead us toward what we truly need.

Bill

City of the Angels, California

I am a musician and angel lover from times dating back longer than memory will lend. I'm a fan of the baseball team also. One of my favorite activities is watching the angels draw symbols, faces, and even other angels in the clouds. Their best work is usually at sunset. I can use these pictures and symbols as angel language, and sometimes they just come right out and speak to me! Either way, I always find angel answers to my present dilemmas.

The angel story I will relate to you happened one night on a lonely drive home, from an even lonelier gig of very poor attendance at the club where I play. This particular day had started out on the wrong leg from the word *go*. I was definitely hammering thumbs instead of nails. Anyway, I was driving home feeling just plain empty, when suddenly I had a sense that my angel friends were circling my car as I drove. Seconds after this realization, my mood changed to that of an expectant child at an amusement park. My angels started snickering, and one shouted out, "All you need is a little applause!" At that moment, the clapping started. Had I not been driving, I would have taken a bow, but I did throw in, "Thank you very much—any other requests?" Imagine, a flying ovation on my drive home—the biggest applause of the night.

Healing Experiences

4

This section describes all types of experiences regarding healing. We heal ourselves every day of something or another. The healing may simply be when we figure out a positive way to solve a problem or make it through a trial with hope. Each individual on the planet has a purpose. Sometimes our purpose is to heal a part of our souls we have lost touch with. Healing can involve resolving an illness or a relationship, a negative thought program that works against us, or guilt and resentment. Mostly healing involves renewing love for ourselves and realizing that we hold the light of God within our hearts. Sometimes we forget to take care of ourselves as a precious vessel of God's love-light. When we bring the angels in on our healings, we will discover that most of all healing is a process of falling in love with ourselves.

Angels comfort us in their own creative ways when we require healing. Comfort becomes a theme in this section. Comfort is peace, contentment, and acceptance. It is defined in the dictionary as relief of suffering or grief.

The most powerful healing tool is forgiveness. Forgiveness has the most powerful effect when it seems impossible. Forgiveness may not happen completely, or all at once, but the moment you become willing just to live and love yourself, willing to forgive whatever has happened to you in your lifetime, a sense of freedom and peace will come over you that truly makes you at one with the angels.

Sol Ta Triane

California

About Healing and the Angels

Did you know angels are the source of physical, mental, and emotional healing energies? I was able to see that this was true years ago when I developed clairvoyance, the ability to see the angels and also other subtle beings.

A local healer named Brother Jesse is known around my neighborhood to have quite a powerful hug, and I don't mean to say that he squeezes you really hard. His hug has some special properties to it. One day when Brother Jesse hugged a person in one of his nontraditional church services, a long white angel appeared and linked into Jesse's body. It looked quite odd, like a glowing tall white pillar of light about four feet wide, suspended diagonally down from fifteen feet above his head. The angel's light then poured in through the back of Jesse's chest, out the front of the chest, and finally into the person he was embracing. The angel seemed to be linked upward into the light and out of sight. It left as quickly as it came. From this experience, I started to realize what healing was all about. I soon found that healers never, ever, work alone.

As we connect to the angelic self, the "God within," we discover that we each have invisible friends and magical healing abilities, and that we are only beginning to learn how to use them. Our sincere and continuous prayer for the healing and transformation of our planet and ourselves will magnetize the best people and spiritual forces that we will need to expand our capabilities so we can help our sisters and brothers.

My initial contact with higher forces began in a meditation for world service. I made no effort to make contact; they came to me as a complete surprise. And now I am involved full-time in spiritual healing work. I travel around the country giving Angel Intensives, a training course for people who want to grow and become healers, too. I also knew even when I was a child that I could be a "healer," but in our "keep-your-hands-off" world it took me until recently to open to my healing capabilities. Would you like to be a vehicle for healing and transformation?

You may ask yourself this question: Is there a loving healer inside of you that wants to come out and take a stand. Yes, you *can* do it. May you open to your inner healer; we need you!

Love is the very foundation of all healing work. Mother Teresa has said that we Americans are the most love-starved people in the world. Let us each find the courage to love. Once you have created a foundation of true selfless love and apply it in your life, you will find yourself secretly being given greater capabilities than you ever thought possible—through the cooperation of the healing angels.

Scarlet Colantoni
South Africa

I have always prayed to my guardian angels and was so happy to find your book. I have had ovarian troubles for fifteen years and I prayed to the healing angels St. Raphael and St. Michael. One day I closed my eyes in deep prayer, and a red light of an intense nature surrounded me. After a while a small flake fell onto me, and I did not know where it had come from. I tasted it, and it was sweet. Immediately I went inside because I thought it looked like a wheat-germ flake. It was, and I knew I had an answer, I was to take a teaspoon of wheat germ daily. Well, the change in my ovaries is incredible.

God and all the heavenly beings—namely Our Lady, all the saints, and angels—have helped me so much. I lost my first child at birth—no reason—in 1979. Then in 1981 my little boy died at the age of one and a half. The doctors used me as a guinea pig and removed most of my thyroid. I believed in God and asked him to help me, and I now have two beautiful children, ages eight and five. I prayed and believed. I am now off drugs for hypertension, and my thyroid, the little that was left behind after my operation fifteen years ago, is starting to work. So, God willing, another miracle.

At thirty-seven years of age, I can say I am truly starting to experience the wonderment of life and the gift that it is. The spiritual guidance and growth have given me so much joy! I look forward to each day and hope all the people of the world will experience and accept the comfort of their guardian angels.

L. Adams

Daytona Beach, Florida

The angels have become very much a part of my daily life and have brought me boundless insight, growth, and comfort.

Six months ago, I went for a mammogram and the doctors discovered a small spot. They weren't sure what it was and advised me to have a biopsy. Reluctantly, they said I could have a six-month follow-up mammogram as another alternative. I was a basket case for a week, and then I decided for the six-month follow-up. I had a couple of reasons for choosing this option. First, I felt that this was an indication to me of further growth I needed in giving my daughter more love. So I committed myself to work in that area. Second, I knew that in six months I would be attending a workshop by the Elisabeth Kübler-Ross Center on healing my inner child. I wanted to give myself the opportunity to do more inner work before considering a biopsy.

Yesterday, I had my six-month follow-up, and the doctors don't understand why nothing showed up on the mammogram! Of course, they had scientific explanations and theories, but I know what really happened! I felt the presence of the angels very strongly yesterday. Two or three times, I heard the fluttering of wings to reassure me they were near and that there were many of them. Elisabeth told us in the workshop that *we are never alone*. She said there are angels all around us, and the harder our lives are, the more angels we have with us. Every day in the workshop, we started off with a moment of silence. That's when I called all the angels in to be near us and work for our highest good. The workshop was a profound and life-changing experience for me, and I am feeling a lot of inner work being done every minute of the day. By the way, my three little angel birds, Rascal, Kisha, and Lucky, continue to teach me all kinds of lessons on love, tolerance, patience, and forgiveness. My angels know how to reach me through my birds to help me discover the lessons I need.

73

Pat Thompson

Stanley, Virginia

This happened about eleven years ago. My uncle Bill had terminal cancer. He'd done fairly well with the illness until he started chemotherapy and went steadily downhill after that. Shortly before he went into the hospital for the last time, his wife, my aunt Molly, awoke early one morning to the sound of laughter and talking. She and my uncle had separate bedrooms at the time. She looked out her window and she saw "three angels walking by, talking and laughing with each other." She never told her husband of this. Then one night after he'd been taken to the hospital, my aunt was reluctant to leave for home because he was so sick. He told her to "go on home and not to worry about him. That he was never alone. There were always *three* others with him."

Uta Nordean

Victoria, British Columbia, Canada

My husband and I have always, more or less jokingly, talked about our "guardian angels" but have never researched this on a deeper level. This last February, I was told I had breast cancer, and while dealing with this shattering news I felt that someone was always present, standing behind me. It was very comforting. A week later I went to a bookstore and saw your book. While going through chemotherapy, I prayed to the angels and visualized hundreds of little angels going into my veins. Presently I'm doing radiation, and again I see little angels coming down with the beam, loading up my cancer cells into little buckets and carrying them out of my body. Often without reason I get an overwhelming feeling of joy flooding my body, and I know my angel is right beside me.

Jamey Shayla Somers
Canada

I have always believed in angels from the beginning of my first memories. I remember as a child of about six that when my parents asked me what I wanted to be when I grew up, I would answer: "I want to grow up, die, and be an angel." Needless to say, my parents were a bit concerned.

I was told once that I have three angels with me all the time, and they are called The Three Sisters. For years I blocked them out, but now I have given them names. I have had a rather difficult and painful life, and I experienced too much heartache; my humor and faith in the angels began to fade. I began to distrust and fear life a great deal. Your book was like a shot of "angel adrenaline" for me.

I was married on Christmas Eve 1990, with hopes of my life finally turning around positively for me. Even my sense of humor was returning because I contemplated wearing wings down the aisle. However, I decided against it, as I didn't think the minister or my husband would have thought it very funny. Four days later, I had a heart attack. I am forty-two years old. I was devastated and in shock emotionally. Then I received your book and read it immediately. It was just what I needed. When I went in for my angiogram to see what damage was done to my heart, I had prepared myself by asking for the help of Raphael, Michael, Uriel, and my highest angel, Angelica.

When I first got to the hospital, I noticed (other than the fact that I was terrified) that I was placed in a fifteen-bed room and was assigned the only bed in the entire ward that had sunshine covering the entire surface of my bed. The rest of the room was dark and gloomy. I envisioned all my angels around me for the rest of the day. All the nurses I encountered were kind and friendly, and I did a lot of laughing that day. Probably the laughter of one who was terrorized, but, what the heck, it was a start!

The end result was that I had no blockages, low blood pressure, and good cholesterol. In short, there was nothing wrong with me. I was very lucky and could go back to 100 percent of my pre–heart attack activities. I was happy beyond comprehension. It all seemed so bizarre to the doctor that he asked me if I was perhaps on cocaine. I laughed out loud and said, "No, nicotine." (I am not on that anymore!) My hospital experience was quite remarkable, and I am very happy to have the angels with me once again.

Paulette

Altoona, Pennsylvania

Change? Did you mention change? All I can say is that I would not care to repeat 1991, although I'm well aware things could have been a whole lot worse. It has been a very difficult year for me to understand. I don't try to understand it now—just accept it. One thing is certain: Without my *faith*, the angels, and the saints, I don't think that I could have made it. My "stone store" folded up—disappointing, but no big deal. But this summer, my young, fun-loving heart had a "spasm" that sent me to cardiac intensive care unit. There was a feeling of aloneness that I have never experienced before. Like total isolation, separation from the entire world. Heart surgery followed, and I am happy to say—ecstatic to say—that last week the cardiologist told me that I am in super, great condition! There are many more changes that need to be made in my life, but that will come gradually. The wonderful part was that the city I live in only has four cardiologists who perform surgery. The angels sent me one who "happened" to be on call that night, who is spiritual and enlightened, and who believes in angels and God! We were on the same wavelength right away. I am so glad I didn't get one of the others! In fact, I think the cardiologist is an angel in disguise!

I have been volunteering at the cancer clinic at one of our hospitals, and I wear my angel T-shirt and a shirt that says "Expect a miracle." The patients like my shirts. Talk about hope and joy—I have never seen as much hope and positive feelings as these patients have! I *loved* your word *changel*—it's great. My life still has *a lot* of changes ahead, but I'm just following it along, curious to see where it's going.

As a child, my "lost" baby teeth were placed not under my pillow, but in the "fairy tree" where the fairies would leave my reward and take my tooth. As far back as I can remember, the fairy tree grew in the "fairy corner" of our yard. My mother firmly believed in fairies and their existence in our yard, so I grew up believing in them, too. The one thing that I didn't take seriously, and I should have, was when my mother told me that the fairies were gone, were no longer in the yard. She was very sincere and sad. A week later my mother died a very untimely and unexpected death; she was in her early forties.

Now I have twin boys who are seven years old and my own fairy garden. Finally, one twin lost his first baby tooth. I had the basket all ready – very small, two inches in diameter, made of twigs and moss. I let him decorate it with flowers, and we put his tooth in it and hung it up in the fairy tree in the middle of the silver star garland. I live in a rent-a-house in the city. The tree came with the yard, and it is such a kind tree. Most people look at me very strangely when I say that. I am not sure what kind of tree it is, but it has a branch that has the shape of a face on it. When the twins find something "special," they always want to stick it on the tree somewhere. So our tree is usually decorated with some pretty wild stuff. Although our house is surrounded by a large hospital and parking lots, in my little fairy haven we have rabbits, squirrels, chipmunks, and birds, and all of them are fairly tame. My flowers and hedge grow like wildfire.

Mary Beth Blanchard
Kauai, Hawaii

[TLT: So that the following letter will make sense, I have included the following excerpt from the June 1992 Angels Can Fly newsletter:

Jo Ann Murphy sent in a powerful forgiveness prayer she knows of to promote quick healing results. Instructions are to repeat it morning and night for at least ten days: Picture the person smiling and send a stream of light from your heart to the person as you say, "(Person's name), I forgive you for anything you have said or done in thought, word, or deed that has caused me pain in this or any other lifetime. You are free and I am free. (Name), I ask you to forgive me for anything I have ever said or done in thought, word, or deed that has caused you pain in this or any other lifetime. You are free and I am free. Thank you, God, for giving me the opportunity to forgive (name) and myself."]

I received your newsletter and really enjoyed it. I have a story to tell and a thank-you to say to you and Jo Ann Murphy.

I am an only child. My mother lived with me for seventeen years prior to 1987, when it became necessary to place her in a rest home due to advanced Alzheimer's disease. I watched her slowly drift away. She hadn't recognized me in three years and had not appeared to hear anything said to her. She only opened her eyes on rare occasions. It was so painful to see her reduced to such a state. I very strongly felt that she was holding on because I might need her. So she clung to life in a body of only sixty-five pounds. Repeatedly, I assured her that I was fine and she could go.

I received and read the newsletter on Saturday, June 20th. I read Jo Ann Murphy's forgiveness prayer and considered it a wonderful idea for future use. On Wednesday, the director of nursing at the home called and said that they thought my mother had pneumonia and they were taking her for a chest X ray, which proved negative. I sat with her and tried to talk her into letting go. No response. On my way home I thought about her and my childhood. My father was an alcoholic, and my mother had so many problems of her own that I became a shadow child. I was somewhat of an afterthought for both of them. I had always put my mother on a pedestal and never blamed her for the things she did or didn't do. About eight years ago, I watched the alcoholism of a close friend, and it swept away the mental block I had in place about my life as a child. The dam broke, and I became very angry and really resented my mother's treatment of me. I have wrestled with these feelings for a long time. I never directly accused my mom, but I know she felt the resentment. I received help from God and my angels and realized that she had done the best she could. I had no right to judge her. Besides, my childhood treatment made a much better mother out of me. By the time I resolved my feelings, she could no longer talk or comprehend my words, so we were never able to discuss these things, much less resolve them.

On Friday morning, as I spoke to God and my angels, the idea of the forgiveness prayer came to me, and I realized that my mother had been holding on all of this time not only because "I might need her," but because she was waiting for my forgiveness and I certainly needed hers. By enlisting angelic assistance, I instantly received the answer and I was also told that she would pass over between the hours of 4:00 and 7:00. I went directly to the home and spoke with her. I said the prayer, and I know she tried to respond as she moved her mouth and mumbled. She did hear me. The area around her bed was filled with beings—I've never felt so many at one time. I sat with her until after 7:00 P.M. At 4:30 A.M. the call came. They said there had been a change in her pulse and breathing, and she would be going within the hour. I didn't even turn on the lamp as I raced across the room with my mind reeling, trying to decide whether or not to wake up my little boy, get dressed, or just throw on a robe. I heard my mother's voice overriding my own thoughts. Clear and strong she said, "Honey, there is no need to come. I don't want you on the road in the middle of the night—it's too dangerous—and don't wake Eddie." I knew she had made the transition, and the clock showed 4:35. I sat down and waited. At 4:40, the phone rang: "Your mom is gone." I asked what time she left. "At 4:35 A.M."

It's still dark, and I'm sitting in my kitchen with pen in hand and coffee on the counter. Thank you and Jo Ann so very much. My mother may have lingered for days had I not received the reminder to forgive and ask for forgiveness. She is now free and dancing with the angels.

Patricia Walton

Paoli, Pennsylvania

I hadn't heard of angel mail before, but since I'm more comfortable with the written than the spoken word, I wanted to try it at once. I wrote a letter to my guardian angel at bedtime and asked her if there was anything she and her friends could do to let my mother-in-law of nearly thirty years know that I loved her. I'd never been able to establish a warm and open relationship with her. Now she was hospitalized, depressed, and terminally ill, and she still seemed to be angry and cold, enclosed within a hard shell.

The next afternoon, for the first time in six weeks, she asked my husband if I was going to come to see her! A few weeks later, she came to our home for her last two months of life, and I was able to give her round-the-clock nursing care. Several times toward the end, as she sat in her chair, she leaned her head over onto my breast and I cradled her for hours as she slept. She had never before initiated an embrace or kiss to her children or to me. She died peacefully, after telling us of seeing "lovely young girls in long pink dresses" who told her they were coming to watch over her. This from a lady who had always preferred the "bah-humbug" approach to life.

One of my most recent blessings from our angels came during an awful day at work. I was feeling very low and dark as I left my desk for about ten seconds. When I returned, a little white feather about one and a half inches long was lying on the floor in front of my chair where I couldn't miss it. When we feel our least angelic, our angels lift us up and love us! My heart sang, and I was reminded that another world exists where love and joy reign. I framed the feather in a heart-shaped frame and keep it on my computer to remind me to climb that ladder and get my head above the clouds where I can see our friends frolicking so heartily that their feathers fall out right into our world!

Allen Le Furgey
Massachusetts

The chapter in Sanaya Roman's book *Spiritual Growth* about nonattachment helped me focus on the bigger picture at a critical time when my father died a few weeks ago. Knowing that all change leads to better things for everyone in the long run and that we have to be willing to let go of the familiar for these changes to come is reassuring and inspiring. I had time to reflect on some of these things I've read on a vacation recently. My perspective has been broadened as a result of my study. To use the terminology of the new spiritual physics, I can say that I've made a paradigm shift in my mind already, although I'm still waiting for the proper time to make a quantum leap. My religious upbringing has been in the Catholic tradition, where they want us to become saints. I can see clearly now, however, that the angelic realm is a higher one to strive for. To paraphrase the words of a popular Billy Joel song, "I'd rather fly with the angels than cry with the saints." I strive to be an angel, and I'm always looking for ways to do so.

Tracy Jenkins
New York

I would like to share my angel story with you. I have only told two other people. Reading your book sparked my memory of it. I'd like to first give you the background so you can see where I was in my life at the time.

I had just gotten out of a very unhealthy, dysfunctional relationship. I was involved with a man who is ten years my senior and was addicted to cocaine. I was codependent. Our highs were very high, and the lows were very low! I thought I could change him, make him stop doing drugs. (Later I learned you can only change yourself!) My self-esteem was zero because all my energy was filtered into him. I would say to myself and others, "I would rather be miserable with him than without him."

Well, the day came when he decided to end the relationship.

It was my twenty-first birthday – what a present. I cried every day for months. All I wanted to do was get back together with him. I did not know I could hurt so much.

I was searching for some help to ease the pain, and one day I picked up the Bible and started to read from page one. I was not brought up with the influence of one particular religion; we just happened to have a Bible in the house. I did not get too far with the Bible. I couldn't really grasp what I was reading at the time. When reading the Bible didn't heal or ease my pain, I started talking aloud to God. You know, asking him the usual stuff.

The night after my "talk," I could not sleep and was crying as usual. That's when I saw her – my guardian angel. At the foot of my bed there was a silhouette of someone with bright, blinding white light surrounding the figure. At first the usual doubts came flooding in – I'm losing my mind, I'm seeing things. The figure did not go away. After I went through my doubts and rubbed my eyes, she began to speak.

She told me everything was going to be all right, that I was surrounded by light and love. She said she was always with me. I felt a warm feeling inside. I felt very loved! I went to sleep, and the next day I was more at peace with myself. It was a wonderful experience!

I now realize that the relationship was a major turning point in my life. I am thankful to God and my angels for being on this wonderful journey with me called life. It is wonderful to know we all have angels just waiting for us to realize their presence. Recently I was with my friend Shelley's two daughters, and her younger daughter drew a picture of me. The older daughter pointed out that I had an angel over my head in the drawing. The little girl saw her — my angel! It was such a special moment. I felt all aglow afterward. I recently introduced my friend Kirsten, a painter, to your book. She had one of her students over and was showing her the book when the phone rang. The caller asked to speak with Angel. Kirsten told him he had the wrong number, not realizing the connection until she had hung up the receiver. I'm sure he had the *right* number.

Simple but Powerful Messages

5

The angels are miracle workers, but if we don't expand our idea of what a miracle is, we may miss the most powerful miracles they bring to our lives. Of course, we won't really miss the lesson or message of our miracles; it just may take longer to realize them if we are caught up in the outside world. In a recent conversation with my friend Shannon, we decided that the type of angel experiences we like the most are the ones in which angels brighten up people's lives and change their perception. Maybe they haven't had a good laugh or a reason to smile, and have been generally depressed. Then they open to the angels and find an almost instant transformation from doom and gloom to light and love. It is exciting to read about amazing rescues where help came out of nowhere, such as when someone gets into a serious accident and is saved by an angel. This is great, but, as Shannon said, maybe if the person had opened up to the divine gifts that the angels have in abundance for us, gifts that lighten our minds and body, the accident wouldn't have happened in the first place. Can we count all the accidents that didn't happen?

What happens to us when we ask the angels into our life? Life becomes more meaningful. My favorite angel movie is The Bishop's Wife, made in 1947, starring Cary Grant, Loretta Young, and David Niven. This movie relays much angelic wisdom; it provides a great example of what happens to humans when they ask God for angelic assistance. The bishop has become quite popular with the wealthy members of his parish and has become obsessed with building a new cathedral. He prays very hard to make this come to pass, so God sends him an angel (Cary Grant) to help things along. I don't want to give the whole story away, but suffice it to say that the bishop receives what he really needs—a realization of what is really important in life. When it is time for the angel to leave, all the characters' perceptions have changed. They don't have an exact memory of the angel's physical presence in their lives. Angels have an ability to veil our perceptions when necessary. When you ask God for something and ask the angels to help you create this something, you may not get the exact something you want, but you will get what every human heart really desires: love, happiness, joy, grace—the angelic gifts that bring meaning into our lives.

When a simple encounter with someone changes your outlook on life to the positive, or when you realize you are seeking wisdom above all else and can find it in simple ways here on earth, these are true angel miracles! When I talk about human angels or angels of the moment, I'm referring to a person who shows up just in time to help someone advance in his or her spiritual growth. The event usually has a distinct message. Messages may be universal, such as "We are all one with God, and therefore must respect one another." Or the message could be personal: "Love yourself as a true child of God." A question arises: Is this a real angel who materialized in human form, or is it a person who became his or her higher self (guardian angel) for a moment to guide another person? I ask: Does it matter?

Regardless of the circumstances in your life, the tragedies, hardships, illnesses, and other trials will always have a silver lining. Somewhere within the situation, the angels are waiting to remind you that you hold the power to change anything into a "positive," simply by the way you think about it and respond to it. In this section, the letters bring into view how the angels guide us toward the positive and provide opportunities that give us a poignant and transforming message at just the right time in our lives. Be aware of where *the message is coming from; detailed instructions that could interfere with our free will are never from angels. Listen closely and attune your heart and mind to the highest vibrational level in the universe—God.* To listen *means to make an effort to "wait alertly" in order to hear something.* Are you listening? If so, to whom?

Shannon

Venice, California

Recently, I was in a situation where I led a committee that had a lot of disagreement among the members. It was unpleasant and frustrating trying to facilitate our task and keep the peace with certain members.

One afternoon during all this, after some difficult phone calls, I threw myself on the bed for a nap. As often happens, my mind started wandering around in that strange twilight area between waking and sleeping. Before I realized what I was doing, I had created a sort of composite of a woman in the field of vision behind my eyes. The picture and thought were dark and murky, and she was somehow made up of the various negative qualities I observed in the committee members. Then, having her trapped in my field, from a higher seat in my mind, I began to examine and criticize her as if she were a specimen and I could reengineer her. Again, I will mention that I really hadn't *consciously* invented this fantasy, but fell into it from the base negativity I was feeling. Well, just as I was getting more involved in this strange thought, I heard a sweet and strong angelic voice say: "We do not do that."

91

Suddenly I was wide awake and slightly breathless from the shock of returning so quickly. My feelings were running wild with the realization of what I had been doing, and my first response was guilt and embarrassment. But these feelings faded as soon as they arose. Then I had a calm understanding that this admonishment was gentle and caring, spoken to me as a well-loved child, telling me that I was in the company of angels now, and that *we* do not need to resort to dealing with things in a negative manner. She conveyed so much to me in that miraculous moment that there was no need for psychology on my part; the experience was purely spiritual.

After that, the issues of the committee lost their intensity for me, and finally when the project was finished, we all agreed that we had done a beautiful job. So, I thank this motherly angel for her guidance and the relief from the illusion of too much responsibility.

Allan P. Duncan
Burlington, New Jersey

I've experienced many miracles in my life. I'm a former highly decorated police officer who for many years only experienced the darker side of life. All I saw was violence, anger, death, and despair, and it affected me deeply. I lost my faith in God on March 28, 1975. It was Good Friday, and I was involved in a gunfight with a psychopath who ended up shooting three police officers, two of whom were killed. I watched the wounded officers bleed to death since there was no way to save them. I remember being barricaded behind a tree, crying and feeling both helpless and useless. I wondered how God could allow such a thing to happen on Good Friday.

I couldn't accept reality as I experienced it, so I sought refuge in a bottle. Within several years, I was a hopeless alcoholic. I was in and out of state mental hospitals, detox, and rehabs. I ended up homeless, living in the woods. I seriously attempted suicide several times, and yet I couldn't die! I was involved in a car accident in which my car was ripped in half, and yet I lived and through all this I wondered why I couldn't die.

I've been sober ten years, thanks to the help and love of many angelic souls. They loved me when I couldn't love myself, and they nurtured me back to health. I realized that there had to be a higher power that had protected me through my dark times, and I sought that power. I realized that there had to be a reason for me living through my hell and that there must be a purpose for me being alive. It was through a support group for recovering alcoholics that I made peace with God and found my way back to the spiritual path.

Today I'm a social worker, working with emotionally disturbed children. I am also a musician, poet, and painter. I have a show in New Hope now of my paintings, and it's receiving rave reviews. One of my paintings is a portrait of the Dalai Lama. I was blessed by him in 1984, and I'm doing work with the U.S. Tibet committee to help free his country. Holy men from India and Tibet have been coming to the show not knowing what was there, and the owner of the gallery said he has never experienced anything like this before. The holy men stated that they were drawn to the gallery and then discovered my paintings. One of them left me a gold Buddhist pendant personally blessed by the Dalai Lama before he returned to India. I am starting a series of angel paintings now.

For Christmas my friends all gave me angels, and I have them all over my bedroom. I made an altar of Buddhas and angels, and I place my angel mail beneath a large Buddha. I burn rose incense and listen to "Angel Love" by Aeloiah while I write my letters and then meditate daily before I go to work. The past several months have been magnificent since I have brought the angels into my practices.

Some of my favorite quotations are: "The difference between a stumbling block and a stepping-stone is how you use it" and "Pain is the touchstone to all spiritual growth." In my life, this has been true. I look back on my painful past as a great learning experience, and realize that I wouldn't be where I am now if I hadn't experienced my personal hell.

Mechelle
Georgia

Guess my letter got hidden away and forgotten for a reason. Life's been a little downhill lately, and I was doing some intense praying over a couple of problems. I started thinking about people receiving roses as a sign or answer to something, and I thought, Well, that is nice, but I need an angel. Please send me an angel!

So here comes your little note with two beautiful angel cards. It had slipped my mind that I had written to you. I was letting myself get too muddled up with problems. What is really ironic is that my problems concerned my children. I have two, and one of the angel cards depicts a boy and girl with their guardian angel watching over them. I have a boy and a girl. I received your note and gift yesterday, and today is Mother's Day. Here I sit alone; neither one of my children has called, but it doesn't matter.

I've had several things going on the last few weeks—a lot of thoughts, and one that I really seemed to dwell on: that I had lived my life for my children and this is what they do in return. I have been a single parent for years, I never received child support, and I had a terrible childhood myself, so I really did work harder and probably gave more to make up for all I didn't have.

Today is a special Mother's Day. Your gift brought it all together. Today I have the answer, wisdom, knowledge, and a *true sense of peace.* I realize that I brought two little souls into this world, that they served a purpose in my life, and that now they have a path of their own to follow. I can't protect them from learning from their own mistakes, and I realize that they'll always be protected by their guardian angels, just as I was, and continue to be.

The Reverend Patty Farr
New York

The angels continue to lighten me up when I become overly serious about my journey, and they strengthen me to carve out new paths in my ministry for Christ, sometimes urging me into places "where angels fear to tread"! As you say, their messages and their presence are always so encouraging, empowering, and full of the most gentle, unconditional love—providing healing balm when I get too intense, serious, and anxiety ridden. They even manage to get me laughing out loud while I sit in meditation these days. My two girls, ages nine and six, think I'm crazy, but they love it. Of course, they have no problem believing in angels. In fact, to me they have always seemed like earth-angels — and very mischievous ones at that.

Excerpt From a Sermon Titled "Friends in High Places"

I remember about a month after my Dad's death, on Sunday morning, when I was preaching at the worship service, I happened to glance down at an unfamiliar face in one of the pews. The man in the pew smiled back at me with the most beatific grin. He looked uncannily like my father, and he was dressed just the way my father used to dress, in a casual pullover sweater, when golfing or playing tennis. After the service was over, this man came through the line to shake hands. He held my hand in his for a long time. We looked at each other closely, and I could feel tears stinging the edges of my eyes. "You remind me of my father," I said cautiously. He smiled that wonderful smile again, and said, "Well, I'm just passing through. As a matter of fact, I'm on my way to play tennis right now." With that, the stranger left the church, and I never saw him again. Many times since that day, I have found myself thinking back gratefully to that man's presence in church that morning and what a lift it gave me. I am now convinced that whether or not he was a human or simply appeared so, he was also definitely an angel.

Many of us will probably live out our entire lives without ever giving serious thought to the possibility of angels. But just as you rely on loving family members and friends to support you when you are going through a hard time, so you can also rely on the angels if you wish, for they, too, are your family, in the spiritual realm.

Native Americans have a very beautiful way of understanding this. They refer to our journey on earth as our walk on the red road. But there is also another road, they say, called the blue road; this is the road of spirit, where our ancestors live. Native Americans believe that for every human companion we have here on the red road, we also have an invisible companion on the blue road, accompanying us while we make our earth walk. Truly we are surrounded by support! As the author of Hebrews tells us, " . . . since we are surrounded by so great a cloud of witnesses, let us also lay aside every weight and the sin that clings so closely, and let us run with perseverance the race that is set before us, looking to Jesus the pioneer and perfecter of our faith" (Hebrews 12:1–2).

Maeve Cooper
Iowa

As I read your book, I was able to recall immediately times in my life when I had encounters with human angels. I could remember every single detail of the meetings, but most important of all, I remember everything that the angels taught me. I wanted to share one encounter with you because it marked a turning point in my life.

Twelve years ago, I was six years into an abusive relationship with my son's father. It was mostly mental abuse, as I was a very insecure person and this man used it to manipulate me.

He was very mean and possessive, and I didn't have a lot of personal freedom in this relationship. Being overweight all my life and teased for it unmercifully as a child, I really believed that there was no way that I could ever attract a decent man. I thought I didn't deserve a decent man because I was ugly. So I settled for what I could get. When we would argue and I would talk about breaking up, this man would tell me, "You know you can't break up with me. You'll never find a man who will want you because there aren't very many men who like heavy-set women." Of course, I believed this.

In 1981 I became pregnant. At first, things seemed to improve between us, but as it got closer to the time for the baby to be born, he went back to being the same mean person. You see, during this pregnancy, my looks changed drastically. My hair grew long and silky, and my complexion became crystal clear. I actually lost weight during the first seven months, but the baby kept growing. It seemed he was using the excess fat of my body, and so I began to slim down, except, of course, where the baby was. This became a threat to this man, I realized later, with the knowledge that he was even more insecure than I was.

When in my ninth month, about to explode, I was standing in the corridor at work waiting for an elevator. A male customer approached me. Since I work in the corporate offices of a department store, I assumed he wanted information on where to find something. He was a nice-looking man and while he wasn't dressed shabbily, he seemed a little out of place in our store. This is what he said to me: "Excuse me, miss, I can see that you're with child and though you don't have a ring on, I'm sure that you have a male friend in the picture. But I just had to let you know that you are looking exceptionally lovely today – just absolutely glowing."

I was so shocked, all I could manage to do was to mutter a weak thank-you. He wished me a nice day, then went around the corner toward the infant's department. A funny feeling came over me, and I knew I had to go after him. No more than ten to twenty seconds had passed, but when I went around the corner, he had disappeared without a trace. Upon asking the sales clerk, I learned that apparently I was the only one who had seen him.

At the time, I didn't know he was an angel, but what he said to me never left me. In fact, it brought about a change in me. It was an instant realization that the man in my life had been lying to me; there would be men out there who would think I was attractive. Most important, I realized that I didn't have to stay with him anymore and put up with his abuse. I was not stupid, ugly, or any of the other things he said about me. Our son was born and though things were somewhat more mellow, I just felt in my heart that I was not where I was meant to be. On the baby's first birthday, I began to make plans to leave him, and three months later I did. It has been a long, sometimes hard road since then, financially and otherwise. After meeting my angel, many times the self-doubt would creep back in, but I have never forgotten the good news he had for me that day, and I will be forever grateful to him for helping me when I needed it. I remember that this angel had the most beautiful, gentle eyes that seemed to say to me, "You are all that you need to be, and you deserve more than what you have." I am proceeding at the pace that is best for my highest good, with my angels beside me helping. I am at the point in my personal path where

I will finally put to rest all the self-doubt and learn to give to myself and love myself unconditionally. I am learning to feel and hear my guardian angel Rita and my spiritual guide Chastity, who helps me learn about myself. Chastity is Native American, and I tease her about her name, but I know it represents an aspect of myself that she is trying to help me with.

It has been such a boost to my self-esteem to realize that I have been blessed with the gift of spirituality, psychic intuitiveness, and direct communication with my angels. I am blessed to know and finally believe that I am special in God's eyes and that I am deserving of all the good that he has in store for me. The best part is knowing that I only have to ask him and the angels for what I need.

Kathy Lynn Klinger
Fort Wayne, Indiana

My angels are always apparent in my life. When I was eight and a half months pregnant and had a twenty-month-old, my husband had been laid off from work and severely depressed for eight months. We had what appeared to be *no* money. His unemployment had run out, and we had bills and no food. On the way home from the OB, my husband kept saying we had no money and I kept telling him that God would always take care of us, that I didn't know how, but I knew that he would.

When we got home, in the mail was a bank statement showing that money had been deposited in our account. My husband was sure it was a mistake, and I didn't want to spend money that was not ours, so I called the bank. They assured me that someone had come in and asked that it be put in our account and that we should feel free to use it. So, we could eat. God had blessed us.

Several months later, my husband got back to work, and we received a phone call from the bank saying that they had just found out the money was put in the wrong Michael Klinger's account. They knew I had called, but the error had just been found. They were sorry and asked if we could pay back the money a little at a time. Well, now of course we could, because my husband was working. So angels can even arrange loans when no one else can!!

Terry Lynn Taylor

Two of my beginning angel lessons involved older African-American men. I will tell you about one of these experiences, which happened in December of 1986. I have only told a few people of this experience and have not written it down until now.

I was living in Virginia and decided to take a long vacation to California to visit my family for the holidays. Since I was giving myself extra time, I thought it would be fun to take the train across country. I didn't realize it would be a lot more than fun.

I was to change trains in Chicago, at which time I would have an economy sleeper room, but from Virginia to Chicago the rooms were all booked, so my first night was spent in a regular seat. If you have ever traveled by train, you know that the train makes stops throughout the night at various cities. During the night, I would dose off to sleep but wake up whenever the train stopped so I could look at the people in the train station and notice who was boarding the train. It was a great "slice of life" to observe. Around 4:00 A.M. the train stopped, and I woke up and noticed a man coming on the train in the car where I was. At this time every window seat in the car was taken, and every aisle seat was empty. For some reason, I was convinced by looking at this man that he had probably been up with his friends all night playing poker and smoking cigars and therefore would most likely smell like cigars and beer. (Now remember I had been asleep, so these thoughts were in my half-conscious mind; that is, they ran deep.) So I decided he better not choose to sit in the empty seat next to me. I figured he probably wouldn't, since there were so many to choose from, but just in case I started to chant in my mind: "Please don't sit here, please don't sit here." Well, guess what? He sat down right next to me. I suddenly experienced an instant feeling of peace and comfort, the best part being that he smelled wonderful. I quickly fell back to sleep with a warm, glowing feeling and woke up in time to catch an incredibly beautiful sunrise full of angelic clouds and streams of light. One of the first things that hit my mind is how prejudiced I had been a few hours before, caught off guard in a semiconscious state, realizing I must now accept this part of me and learn a lesson from this experience. The man, I'll call him Ray, whom I didn't want to sit next to me for ridiculous reasons, was still sitting next to me, and I was glad.

Ray was awake and watching the sunrise with a most pleasant smile on his face. We sat quietly looking out the window as the train moved through a part of town racked with poverty. Morning had broken, and I decided to listen to my portable cassette player. I put a tape by George Winston on, titled, appropriately, "December." Through my headphones, I heard the wonderful piano music as I watched houses go by that I was sure no one could possibly live in, considering their run-down condition. The song "Some Children See Him" began playing, which is my favorite on that tape. For some reason, it sounded more wonderful than usual as I noticed a most precious sight. In the upstairs window, in a house I was sure had been abandoned, I saw the beautiful shining face of a little boy as he pulled open the curtains to watch the train go by. He had curly golden blond hair and a smile that blasted me with love, hitting deep in my heart. I was sure I had seen an angel of God. All the while, this wonderful song about children was playing in my ears as my senses heightened, leaving me again with a sense of peace and love for all humanity.

Ray left to go eat breakfast, and as I watched him I realized what a different perception I had of him now. We still hadn't spoken, but I felt as if I knew him in some way. About five minutes later, I went to have breakfast and ended up sitting next to him. Now I was able to see him interacting with other people and noticed he had a gentle voice and warm smile. People sitting with us felt very comfortable telling him all sorts of things about themselves, their travels, and so forth, and he listened attentively.

The train arrived in Chicago, and I changed trains. On the new train, I had my own little room. This was great because I could go out and wander about the train, then go retreat in solitude and read. On one of my trips out to the observation car, I discovered there was only one seat left, and it just happened to be right next to Ray. Ray was on this train, too. So I took the seat. A mother was coming up the aisle dragging a little boy behind her, and when they got to Ray, the little boy blurted out, "Look at my new ring," reaching his little hand out so Ray could get a good look. The mother was a little startled, thinking that maybe her child was bothering someone, but Ray's reaction was so kind and he made the little boy feel so special that she just smiled and relaxed. After this episode, I remembered the song "Some Children See Him" and saw God as I looked at Ray.

Finally, we had a conversation. I asked him where he was going, and he said to the Los Angeles area to stay with his daughter and his grandchildren for the holidays. He told me some wonderful things about his family.

That night I wandered into the club car and sat down with three other people at one of the tables. Across from me were two African-American women. Directly across from me was a woman who had grown up on the streets of Chicago. Sitting next to her was a young woman who had lived a very comfortable life. Next to me was a white man in his twenties who was "into" body building, and then there I was. Just for the record, I have long blond hair and blue eyes, and people think I look fairly innocent, although I assure you I was not born yesterday. The four of us decided to play a game of spades. My partner was the woman from the streets of Chicago. She wasn't exactly pleased with me as her partner, but I tried not to be affected by it. The game got going, and my partner and I started winning and became instant friends, really playing in synch and having a great time. Not much else was happening in the club car that night, so our card game attracted a small crowd standing around us — including some of the people who worked on the train. They cheered the game on, and we were all having a great time. I felt a wonderful sense of peace again, and I noticed Ray standing in the background with his wonderful smile. His presence made me feel safe, as if I had a longtime friend traveling with me, watching me have fun.

The rest of the train ride was great. I met many friendly people whom I would laugh and talk with. When I got to California, I reflected on the train trip and on Ray. I began to see a pattern when Ray was around. I couldn't help but think that he was a manifestation of my guardian angel. Or simply a very angelic human who brought magic wherever he went and secretly sprinkled it around so people would have fun and get along with one another in profound ways. I am not sure I was able to put in words the truly deep impression that trip made on me. There are always so many subtle incidents that happen when the angels are around that are difficult to put into words. All I know is I will never forget Ray, and I gained a new awareness regarding issues of prejudice and of the unity of all people. In fact, a few years later, after a series of synchronisms, I found myself working with children in a racial integration program in the Los Angeles school district, where I met some of the most incredible teachers – the children.

Melinda Thiessen

California

When I saw your closing note that you are collecting angel stories, I felt compelled to pass one along. It happened in San Francisco, when I'd spent a beautiful summer day in my own company amid thousands of visitors at Ghirardelli Square.

I love blending in with the background and watching the movie of life play out in front of me.

As I was walking back to my truck in the golden, unearthly light of the setting sun after a beautiful, peaceful, and fulfilling day, I met a smiling old African-American man sitting on a park bench reading the paper. As I walked past, he put down his paper, and we smiled at each other. His crinkly smile formed a warm, sunny bridge that effortlessly united us in a timeless moment despite the differences in age and skin color. He said to me, in a husky voice with a touch of a Southern accent, "Child, there's more light shining out of your face than is shining onto it from the sun. You're glowing. You must have had a wonderful day because the joy is glowing out of you like a sunrise. You are happy because you're doing what you're supposed to be doing, and that makes the people around you happy, too!"

Wow, he didn't look like any of the angels I've seen described, but I know my wrinkled old smiling friend is an angel, delighted with himself for fooling everyone else he met that day!

Dotti Wheeler

Sonoma, California

I thank you for pointing out in your book that it is indeed possible for angels to come up to people in unusual places — like bars. Several years ago, when I was going through a difficult time in my life, I had just such an experience.

The angel called herself Judy, and she advised me not to share this story with people because they might "put it down" since the experience took place in a bar. I am not now, nor have

I ever been, a heavy drinker. At the time of this event, I worked a 4:00 P.M. to midnight shift at a 7-11 store. I had no car and was renting a small bedroom connected to a somewhat seedy restaurant/bar. I was having dizzy spells at the time that no one knew about. Judy did know and told me not to worry about it; she said it had something to do with the Holy Spirit. She also told me I had absolutely no idea how much God loved me and how precious I was. This part has made me cry every time I have related this story to anyone. She told me that I should stop repeating my prayers, that I had already been heard. She said I shouldn't try to "outline" how the things I wanted were going to come about. She said God wanted far more for me than I could ever think to ask for.

She also told me I would forget about my conversation with her, which was wrong—I'll never forget it. I was told I should always remember to give the credit to God and not let my ego take credit when "the changes" took place in my life. Judy also told me that there would be a time of darkness before things got better. Darkness indeed! About a year later I woke up in the hospital with my eyes bandaged after an eye operation. She encouraged me to hang onto the light at the end of the tunnel when I hit this difficult period of my life and said it was extremely difficult to translate heavenly time to earth time, and she didn't want to be pinned down as to when these changes would take place. By the way, the bar was a funky neighborhood bar, with only regular customers; very few strangers came in. She was dressed in a gray suit with a white blouse, prim and proper looking, like a schoolteacher or librarian. Very out of place in there!

It has been about seven years now. I feel I have experienced the bad part, but not the good so far. Two summers ago I spent three months living in my car—a very bleak time in my life. I would love to read other stories of people's unusual encounters with the angels.

Tom McClellan
Ontario, Canada

When I was about twenty, on my own, without any definite goal—having given up my conviction to become a Carmelite monk—I was sitting on the bank of the Detroit River, in Windsor, contemplating my future, asking God to give me a sign. I tried to meditate but got a general blank, so I decided to hitchhike back to my flat. The first car that pulled over was driven by a junior navy officer, and he was wearing his white uniform. He started telling me that when he was younger he didn't really know what he wanted to do, but things seemed to work out as he did what seemed right at the time.

There was something strange about this naval officer; he was obviously not rich, but very much at peace with himself, calm and self-assured. I really felt at the time that God had answered me through this sailor. I thought it was strange that Canada doesn't have any naval presence on the Great Lakes, except on rare occasions, and that this sailor driving an old car happened to be driving on Riverside Drive when I needed a ride. I had always admired navy men, and as a little boy wanted to be a navy pilot. After reading your first book, I deeply believe that this navy man was really an angel who came to answer my prayer.

A few years ago when I was working at Miracle Food Mart, a grocery store, I was wondering if I was doing what God had intended for me in this life. As I was driving to work at night, I saw a purple streak go across the sky and then explode as if a meteor had hit the ground. I was driving out in the country at about 11:30 P.M., and there were no reports of this later.

Just a few days ago I was wondering if I was going to develop enough love to be the person I ideally want to be. I was wondering if it was possible. At that moment, a flock of about twenty doves appeared from nowhere and flew over me.

Suzanna Solomon
Washington, D.C.

[TLT: I interviewed Suzanna for "The Angel Forum" in Messengers of Light, and I had lost touch with her after she moved and hadn't been able to find her. After a series of coincidences, our paths crossed again.]

I sit looking out of the window into the spring day. The bright pink and white blossoms across the way punctuate the gray of this rainy day as I feel the gathering angels' excitement of new and glorious things to come.

Since you interviewed me for the book you were writing about angels, when we both lived in Malibu (1989), I have thought many times about you and your good works. How pleased I was to have found your published book here in Washington, D.C. Many people have come to me to meet their angels because of what you wrote. Within a day or a week after reading your book, they were mysteriously guided to find my ad in the *Pathways Magazine* about meeting and being empowered by one's angels. They felt the synchronism and knew they had been divinely guided.

The angels have brought me to live in D.C. It has been a gloriously intense two and a half years since I first came here. I live on the third floor of my son's beautiful Victorian stone mansion in the middle of the city in a transitional African-American neighborhood. Fire engines screaming with their need of passage and the rumbling of trucks shake the whole house as they pass by. Out-of-work men hang around the corners drinking beer and selling drugs. A far cry from beautiful Malibu, but in spite of it all, my home is a heavenly sanctuary filled with the presence of angels and light, and I feel at home here.

A few months ago, I went to the supermarket with a friend of mine. We were both very tired after sight-seeing all day. We dragged ourselves into the store to buy food for dinner. As we walked in, I instantly made eye contact with an African-American man putting apples in order. I could not help but smile at him, my Godself leaping out through my tiredness. As we approached him he said, with gleaming eyes and a loving heart, "What's that golden light I see around the two of you? Who are you? I have never seen anything like this before." I answered, "It is our God-light that you see. Out of our oneness, you are able to see through your Godself eyes. Thank you for reminding us that in spite of our human fragility we are also our Godselves bright." With tears in his eyes he said, "Wouldn't it be wonderful if all people could always see and feel each other's God-light, no matter what color, size or shape, no matter male or female, no matter rich or poor? Certainly every thing would be very different." So, now every time I go to the market we connect for a moment or so, and we are uplifted. Indeed, this is my lesson, my purpose for being here in D.C. – to see, to feel, to know the presence of God is in everyone, everything, and everywhere. The sun has just come out, and the wetness twinkles bright in acknowledgment of my own inner brightness in feeling our oneness with the angels.

Kathy Faulstich
California

I can't quite remember exactly when this happened to my husband, Vern. I think it was about fifteen years ago.

For four days Vern kept getting a message several times a day while he was wide awake, at his desk, at work, or watching TV. The message was: "Look for the boy with the rose." Over and over this came to him. He always said his uncle Bud was his "private angel," so he assumed the message was coming from him.

On day four of the messages, Vern went to a coffee shop he hadn't been to in at least five years. He sat at the counter next to a young boy about sixteen or seventeen years old. The boy had a small pastry and a glass of water in front of him, and Vern remarked that someone young and strong needed more to eat than that. The boy gave him a dirty look and said, "_____ off, mister." Vern asked him, "What's your problem, son?" No answer came. Vern asked again, and this time the boy said, "None of your _____ business, mister."

At this point the boy reached for his glass of water with his left hand and Vern saw a tattoo of a rose on the inside of his left arm just below the elbow. Vern knew now that this was the young boy he was to find and help. He started to question the boy again about what was wrong, and finally the boy said, "What's your problem, mister?" Vern said, "I don't have a problem, but you do and I was sent to help you." The boy looked at Vern and said, "What are you, mister, some kind of a nut?" "Yes," Vern replied. "I've been called a nut, and more, lots of times, but I never let it bother me – because I'm a very special 'nut.' I can help people solve big problems in their lives, so you may as well tell me yours because I'm not going to leave here until you do!" The boy said, "Well, no one can help me, not even a nut. My life is one giant mess, and the only way out is suicide and I have a foolproof plan. Want to hear about it, mister?" "No," said Vern. "I just want to know *why*, not *how*."

The boy went on to explain that his parents were his one and only problem (or so he thought). His parents took away his gold earring, his stereo, his car, and his allowance, and insisted he work harder at school, go to church, read one book a month, and so on. He was also required to spend three nights a week at home. Vern tried to keep a straight face during all this explanation, but a smile broke on Vern's face and the boy became even angrier! "It's not funny, mister. My life is hell. I have no freedom at all, I have a year at school to go, and I just can't take it anymore; I'll be better off dead, and then 'they' can live with it – they are killing me!" It was then that Vern got serious and began to put a theory of his into words.

"Let me tell you something way out in left field that may help you. Just listen to me for a few minutes, and then if you still feel the same way, you and I will shake hands and I'll leave, okay?" The boy said, "Okay, but don't preach or yell the way they do twenty-four hours a day!" Vern began to explain one of his very favorite metaphysical theories, and the boy's face turned calm and childlike. "I'm not sure why your parents have set down all these rules – the reason could be love or whatever – but that is not important here." The boy looked startled but kept quiet while Vern continued. "I think you need to realize that *you* picked these two people to be your mom and dad." The boy interjected, "No way, mister. I would never pick out anyone that mean. By the way, how could I have picked them? I wasn't even born when they met. This is crazy; you really are nuts!"

Vern continued, "I believe in reincarnation, and I also believe that between your last life and this one, when you were at rest in the Universe, your soul-spirit (the part of you that never dies) looked around for a set of earthly parents. You needed one male and one female to come together so you could have a vehicle of entry for your physical body. Your soul spark took up residence in that body, and here you are. So stop and think of all that hatred you have for this man and woman. You looked down on Earth from the Universe, and you found one male and one female out of all the people on Earth. You liked what you saw, you liked their values, and you started to pull strings from the other side to get these two people together so you could be part of their family in this life. Maybe the next time around you may pick someone different, or you may pick them again. So I'd like you to think about all these bad feelings you have now. Don't you think in view of the fact it was you who picked them out, and not the other way around, that these feelings you have about killing yourself are way off base?" There was a long pause, and, with a certain calm not there before, the boy said, "Mister, you really believe what you just told me, don't you?" Vern said, "Yes, think about the possibility that you chose to be a member of their family. Maybe your friends at school think your parents are too old-fashioned, or maybe you are a headstrong kid who needs a good kick in the pants. Whatever the reason, remember that you liked what you saw from the other side long ago. Go home and take a good look at what you see. Try and talk to your parents this time and listen to them. Ask them to listen to you. If you want me to go with you, I will, but try it—don't look for a miracle right away. Living is hard work for you and your parents, but give them a chance. Work it out, work hard. You can do it. Then, if you feel that it is too tough to live at home, leave when you are eighteen. Join the navy, go to school, live your own life. Remember, you wanted this life; so *live* it, don't *end* it!"

With tears in his eyes, the boy said, "Mister, you are still nuts, but what you said is so far-out it must be partly true. At least you care. Thanks, man." He left the coffee shop, and Vern never saw him again. But I did, on the day I buried Vern. A tall young man in his early thirties came up to me and said, "I had to come today. I wanted to say good-bye and thanks to Vern. He helped me out once, and now I have a beautiful wife and two kids. I still don't get along with my parents very well, but we talk and visit once in a while." I asked, "Who are you?" He said, "The boy with the rose" and held out his arm for me to see.

Parents Write
About Their Children

6

I have always known I had a guardian angel looking out for me. I don't remember when I was first told about my guardian angel, or if it was a human being who told me. My earliest guardian angel memories are of feelings – wonderful feelings of grace, magic, beauty, and a oneness with all the life vibrating in my extra-large backyard. Other memories are of floating to sleep with a golden light that let me know I was never alone. My experience of angels has always been more than just a belief; it is a knowing deep inside that began long before I entered the earth realm. I was born knowing I had an angel with me. You may think, Well, sure, that is easy to say – we can all invent our past however we desire. My confirmation of this knowing comes now through experiences of children I know and stories their parents have told me. A lot of parents are finding out that their children believe in angels, even when they have never mentioned the idea to their children and have no reason to think any other adult has.

I have two nieces and a nephew who have taught me quite a lot about angels, and about joy and hilarity. When I was writing my first book about angels, I asked my nieces to tell me some things about angels. Their answers were great! Jessica, who was four at the time, told me that angels probably glow in the dark and then stated in a confident way, "Of course, we know they have feet." We all laughed hysterically at this statement. Then something very special happened. Elizabeth, who was eight at the time, wrote a poem about angels for my first book and began to read it. When she came to the line that said, "And I know you can't put your hand out and touch them," Jessica, who was listening very attentively, got a strange look on her face and reached her arm out behind her and moved *it around as if she were trying to reach for something in the dark. I had two thoughts: one, she assumed that her angel was standing right behind her all the time, and, two, it never occurred to her that she wouldn't be able to feel her angel with her hand.*

I have found that most children who are aware of angels naturally think of angels as protection, and also that children have their own little worries and fears, and angels help them relieve these fears and worries. If we can teach children about angels in an open, nonfearful, and accepting way, perhaps the patterns of fear and worry that humans seem to incur simply by being on the earth will not be such a problem in their later years. If you are already aware that your children know about angels or if you have told them about angels, reassure them every day that their angels love and protect them. Children are so creative that they will expand their relationship with angels in their own ways. If allowed and encouraged in a positive and simple way, children's relationship with their angels will be a gift for their parents. Children and angels never fail to bring me joy and laughter. Sometimes, just being in the presence of a child or an infant is a true angel experience. A child's angel experience is of such pure nature that it is direct confirmation of the angels' existence. I bet many parents are finding this out today. The following letters are from parents talking about their children and their children's experiences with angels.

Stacy and Tessa Sutherland
California

I have a five-and-a-half-year-old daughter named Tessa. Tessa was trying out for a play at school and had to sing a song. After a while, we decided that she should sing "Itsy Bitsy Spider."

Tessa sang this song with little mishap for one and a half days. However, five minutes before the tryout, she forgot the words to the song. Well, I was rather mortified. After several failed attempts to teach her the song again, I tried to get her to sing "Happy Birthday." She could not remember the words. By the way, Tessa insisted she was not nervous.

Well, I thought to myself, I can either get upset about this situation or just "let it go" and make light of the situation. I chose the latter. I then said to Tessa, "Oh, well, you just go up there and sing whatever comes to mind. Whatever you want to – you'll do just fine." She said, "Okay," and left to stand in line for the tryouts. Meanwhile, I went into a "meditative alpha state" and asked that Tessa's guardian angel guide and protect her at this time. I also asked that Tessa's highest good be done.

Tessa got up in front of at least thirty people standing tall and proud – smiling beautifully and radiating light. She sang in a clear and loud voice with perfect pitch the following: "One little, two little, three little angels. Four little, five little, six little angels. Seven little angels here!" Needless to say, she got a lot of applause and I was astounded.

[TLT: In a subsequent letter, Stacy told me that Tessa did indeed get a part in the play – as a munchkin.]

Christina L. Ross
North Carolina

As I was reading the first few pages of *Messengers of Light,* a wonderful synchronism occurred, which I would like to share with you.

119

I have twin daughters named Katie and Amy who are truly blessings from God. They are ten years old, and, without having knowledge of my reading your book, they came to me with a beautiful tale of angel help. Many months went by before they told me their story because they were afraid they would "get in trouble" for being careless. I will relate the experience in the words of Amy as she saw it—her imagery was so enchanting!

Amy: "We were swinging on the swing set out in the backyard and had put our pet rabbits down on the ground to play. As Katie began to swing, her rabbit Priscilla hopped under the swing set where Katie's feet would have touched the ground. Katie said that if she kept swinging high enough, her feet wouldn't kick the rabbit. She was swinging so high she went way above the edge of the garage roof [twelve feet high]. Then Katie's foot got caught on the swing bar [support post] and pulled her out of the swing way up in the air. Then I saw something so magical I couldn't believe it. Katie turned a complete flip [360 degrees] in slow motion and landed on her bottom in the grass, barely missing Priscilla! On each side of her was one boy angel and one girl angel and lots of pretty colors like dark pink and light pink and pale blue and yellow, but I could still see Katie and her clothes through the colors. Where the angels were touching her, on her shoulders and hips, was a real pretty white light and she landed so softly for being so high up in the air. I'll never forget what I saw!"

Well, as you can guess, I was sitting there with my mouth open. Then I had an uncontrollable desire to burst out laughing! Which I did. The girls were so shocked that they weren't in trouble for swinging so high or for putting their rabbit's life in peril that they had tears in their eyes. I told Katie to thank the angels for their help and to consider what might have happened had they not helped her in her carelessness. She explained that even though she couldn't feel them touching her, she knew in her heart everything was going to be okay even though she was falling.

Coincidentally (ha ha), my mother, whom I hadn't talked to for over two months, called the same day, and I related this story to her over the phone. After I finished telling her what her granddaughter Amy had seen, she said, "This is unbelievable! A friend of mine has just left my house, and we have spent the last six hours or so talking about that very subject – angels! I've never given them much thought until now, but you better believe I will in the future." I said, "Mom, the longer I live, the more I realize that things happen for a reason. And ours is not to question, but to be thankful for each and every episode the angels bring to us."

[TLT: I love the way Christina let her children know that it is a good idea to show the angels gratitude for helping them and to use the experience for a positive lesson in life.]

Don Kerr

Washington

What I want to write about is my son Gavin. He is a multiple-handicapped son with Down's syndrome, Klinefelter's syndrome, and epilepsy, who is also partially crippled. He

121

seemingly has three or four strikes against him, but I believe he is of the angelic realm. His whole personality just *shines* with humor, cheerfulness, and love. He never lets my wife and me get into an argument. He steps in and puts an end to our little row. He is at present going to summer day camp for the handicapped, and the counselors up there all fight to get him in their group. They all love him because he is so cheerful and cooperative.

Do you think I have an angel in the house? When I take him to church, the pastor tells me he voluntarily greets people as they come into church. The pastor told me he has given the members of the church a great lesson in love. Isn't that what angels do best?

Terry Lynn Taylor

Don's letter reminded me of a little girl I once knew about. She lived in the same housing complex as I did. I'll call this little girl Jennifer; she was about three years old at the time. Before I got to meet Jennifer, I heard about her from someone familiar with Jennifer's family. I heard about the hardships Jennifer's family faced because of her condition, which I think was caused by spina bifida. She was kept alive by a respirator and needed round-the-clock nursing care. To make matters worse, she could not speak and had limited use of her limbs. Among other things, her condition put a financial drain on her family. So I began to feel very sad for this family.

In time, I got to know Jennifer's older sister and gave a

copy of *Messengers of Light* to her mother. I still hadn't met Jennifer. One day her mother was riding her bike by my house and stopped to say thank-you for the book. She said that she was thinking about angels and that she'd had a discussion with her family, and they all decided that Jennifer was the angel in their family. She said that Jennifer has never shown any type of anger or the meanness that children can occasionally display and that she has the sweetest disposition and has taught the family about love they never knew could be. Also, her mother was studying to be a nurse, so she was introduced into a new career by having Jennifer.

I thought to myself, How special; I would love to meet this child. I also thought how funny it was that I had been feeling sorry for a family who felt they were living with an angel. A day or two later, I was sitting in my living room indulging in a negative mood, upset over something trivial, when I heard a noise outside my window. I looked out the window and saw something I will never forget. Jennifer was going by in her special stroller. The sun was shining on her golden hair, and in each hand she held a dandelion. She had an incredibly beautiful smile on her face as she looked back and forth at her flowers as if they were the most magnificent creations in the universe. She was so full of joy, and radiant light reflected off her pretty face. I felt a blast of love come over me, so intense that tears instantly streamed down my face. I was overtaken with emotion at this scene, and I can assure you that my former mood went out the door and I was left with inspiration and peace in my heart. I later got to meet this beautiful and intelligent little girl, and I would have to agree with her mother – they have an angel in the house!

Joshua G. and Mary G.
Colorado Springs, Colorado/Hinesville, Georgia
Letter 1

I don't know if I should be writing and telling you this. My son Joshua, who is six, has an angel whom he talks to all the time. Joshua met her at the baby-sitter's house. Joshua says her name is Brenda. He told me he is the only one who can see her; she won't let me see her. She goes everywhere with Joshua. Brenda was telling Joshua how his dad was doing when he was in Saudi Arabia during the war. It was so exciting. I knew my husband would be okay! Joshua says Brenda stays in his room now; she was always going to the mountains where she lives. Joshua says Brenda and her family were killed in the mountains. He told me how he talks to Brenda. In his words: "Her mind talks to my mind, and my mind talks to hers. We don't talk the way you and I do."

Letter 2

Everything is going really well for us. Our lives have changed a lot—I would have to say because of Joshua. We had to move to Hinesville, Georgia; my husband got restationed. I was going to send Joshua and his younger brother by plane, and I was going to drive out with my oldest son and three cats. It turned out that we all drove together, but when Joshua thought he was going to fly, he said that Brenda would keep him and his younger brother, Brandon, safe, and that I wouldn't need her because her dad was going to be with me. I said, "Who's that?" Joshua replied, "You know, God." I said, "Fine, I can

124

definitely handle that." The drive from Colorado to Georgia was great, and Brenda watched out for the whole family on the way. The last thing that has to be said is that Brenda wants Joshua to pray a lot, and she prays with him. She has also taken him to a lot of castles. He drew a picture of one, and it looked pretty good. He said almost every night Brenda takes him somewhere.

Eileen D. and Michael D.
California

I have a thirteen-year-old son, Michael, who to my surprise was born on Saint Michael the archangel's day, September twenty-ninth. I was not aware of this until my son was five years old. I was flipping through a book of names and was delighted to find this information listed next to the name Michael. Since the age of eight (to my knowledge), Michael has had a spirit friend, Josh. Michael has on occasion made me privy to Josh's messages, which were 100 percent accurate. The following was one of the most unexpected messages.

I am a nurse who works at a children's hospital with the adolescent and young adult patients. Many of my patients have become my friends, and one of my favorites was Janet. Janet died in 1991. Michael knew I liked Janet; she had been to our house many times. Janet was born with a chronic and terminal illness, cystic fibrosis, which is the number one genetic killer of children. Due to her rigorous health-care regime, her strength of character, and the strides of modern medicine, Janet had triumphantly turned twenty-three. Janet's health condition became critical in June–July 1991. She was hospitalized for weeks. She would seem to get better, only to have her illness recur. I was on a leave of absence during this time, and so I was unable to keep track of how she was doing on a daily basis. Michael and I were busy that summer with music lessons, swimming, and taking care of daily errands. After a very busy morning out and about, Michael and I were driving home listening to the radio, when out of the blue Michael turned to me and said, "Mom, Joshua wants me to tell you something. He says that Janet is much sicker, and she's going to die." I looked at the clock on the dashboard; it was 11:30 A.M. We arrived home at about 12:20 P.M., and there was a message left on my anwering machine saying, "Eileen, this is the hospital. It's 11:30, and Janet has taken a turn for the worse. She has asked to be transported from the intensive care unit to the adolescent unit to die."

Months after Janet's death, I asked a colleague of mine to coauthor an article about Janet. The article included some of Janet's writings combined with our words. The message we wanted to get across was to make health professionals aware of how ill prepared we are to deal with death. The point being that we need to improve our skills, and that people like Janet have much to teach us. Three weeks after submitting our article to a national nursing journal, the editor called to say the magazine would buy and publish our story. The next day at work, I told a fellow nurse how excited I was to get the call of acceptance. She asked me when I had gotten the call, and I told her yesterday. She said, "Eileen, yesterday was Janet's birthday."

Childhood Remembrances

7

Sometimes when we think about the angels' influence in our lives, we begin to recall unexplained situations from our childhood, situations that were so significant the memory is still very clear. I have quite a few of these memories. When I was around eight or nine years old, I remember having some strange experiences, which when I look back seem to have been "mystical experiences." One of them would happen right before I fell asleep. I would be lying on my back with my eyes closed, and a feeling as if I were starting to spin would take over. It wasn't the kind of spinning that makes you dizzy; I just knew I was spinning. Then a vortex would appear above me, full of the most incredible colors I'd ever seen. I would feel myself rising up into the vortex, accompanied by a floating sensation. I would spend a certain amount of time in the vortex. It seemed like a long time, but I don't know if it was. There was no communication by words in this space, but I always felt connected to something definite. The main thing I remember about this experience is that it happened more than once and gave me feelings of pure bliss. It wouldn't happen every night, but when it did, it was so wonderful that for a while I tried to make it happen. Then I started to think that maybe I was doing something wrong, and it stopped.

The other experience I remember from this age happened in a park around sundown. I was walking out of the park with my dad, and I noticed all the trees begin glowing and vibrating. Being a Virgo, I can be a bit of a hypochondriac, so I thought for sure something awful was happening. So I stopped my dad and said, "Wait, Dad, I think I'm going blind. All the trees have strange lights around them." I don't know if my dad remembers this—I haven't asked him—but *he said, "No, you are not going blind," and I reluctantly took his word for it. I also felt a feeling of lightness and a sense that everything was breathing in the same rhythm I was. I could also hear the breathing. The feeling passed, but the situation stayed with me.*

I can't really analyze these experiences, and I'm not sure we're supposed to. I've talked to several people who remember similar events from their childhoods, and they feel the same way. Who knows what, why, and how these experiences take place? They are often called "mystical experiences," and the mystical inspires a sense of mystery. The angels are part of the mystery of life, and sometimes when we try to make sense out of something we ruin it. I have heard it said that logic is us talking to ourselves. If something doesn't make sense to our five senses, I say leave the explanations alone. Why take the fun (angels) out of life's little mysteries? In the words of Sir Thomas Browne, "To believe only possibilities is not faith, but mere philosophy." Faith is powerful positive energy; it can induce physical changes.

Rose Blaney
Oregon

At the age of five, on a sunny day, I was playing at a friend's house. Her mother called her in to eat lunch. I stayed outside alone and seriously injured my ring finger. I was rushed to the hospital, where they sewed it back on. I was to remain there for five days.

Staying there was scary. I was alone and way up on the fourth floor. I missed my family. On the second night, the nurses brought in a baby boy who was very sick, and he would not stop crying. His constant crying comforted me. On the fourth

night, about 3:00 A.M. the baby stopped crying. I was *terrified*.
I didn't know what to do. I was so scared that the baby had
died. I couldn't get out of bed to peek at him. It was very scary
to be alone, terrified, and thinking that the baby had died on
the dark fourth floor of the hospital. My breathing became
harder, and my heart was beating very fast. Then, outside the
window, a brilliant beautiful blue light appeared and floated in
through the window, stopping by the left side of my bed. I felt
no fear! I felt warm and safe, and I began to feel sleepy. I shut
my eyes, hearing a song that told me not to fear, that it would
be all right.

In the morning, the baby's parents got to take him home.
This happened a long time ago. I am thirty-eight now; I was
five then – yet I can still feel that warmth and hear the song just
as if it had happened last night.

Lori Jean Flory (Angelic Name: ALAEYASH)
Colorado

The angels and master teachers started to attune me for
the spiritual work my husband, Charles, and I are doing now,
when I was three years old. It is all a process of growing through
steps and integrating as we go along. Here is what used to happen after I had gone to bed at night. This occurred sometimes
five or six times a night, all throughout my childhood years,
my teen years, my young adulthood, and even now – although
not as much. To begin with, I would hear a bell – a nonphysical
bell – which I sometimes still do hear. The clarity and tone are
unlike anything on our physical earth. Then I would hear a loud

high-pitched frequency in my ear. A feeling of increased vibration would come over me, and it seemed like the frequency would rise to a higher pitch and then come back to where it was before. When this would occur, I would feel as though I were going up and up, and I had no control over it, so I learned to just flow with it. Of course, now I understand what was happening, but then there was no one to explain it to me, so it was a little confusing.

This has happened to me hundreds of times. When I was older, the angels explained that they were working with my frequency and attuning me so that we would be able to work together more intensively when I was older. They stressed that they did not mean to upset me and that we had agreed prior to this lifetime that we would accomplish certain work together.

Since then, I have heard the celestial angelic bells that are nonphysical. I have also heard angelic choirs singing that are more clear and beautiful than any music upon the earth. It has been particularly profound to hear them when Charles and I have been in the Rocky Mountain National Park and deep in meditation in the forest. The celestial music that I have heard rings through the forest, making it seem like the most beauteous chapel on earth.

Many times as the years progressed, in meditation or rest, I would sense these teachers focusing what seemed like laser bursts of light upon my third eye, and I would experience moving through a tunnel with the wind and emerging in a place of inexplicable beauty and gardens. I remember a white arbor with a pathway leading to a garden of roses, a place that must be very special to me when I am in spirit. Then I would be swept back; once I heard a loud voice telling me, *"Go back."* I am healthy, and these occurrences were never a result of an illness.

Now when I experience these laser bursts of light, words of light and sentences of light accompany them in the inner vision. I know that there has always been a higher purpose for all of this, and I think it is part of why I see, hear, and sense the angels. They speak in my left ear, and we have running conversations every day now. Often times at night I will see beautiful lights and auras of white light that light up the bedroom wall. I have always accepted them with the innocence of a child; they are family.

Bea Rowley

Victoria, British Columbia, Canada

Your invitation for us to write you about "signs and wonders" in our experience reminded me of a "sign" I had many years ago that involved clouds.

I was brought up Roman Catholic and so was familiar with angelic and saintly powers and the possibility of miracles.

When I was twelve years old, I was subject to a continuing painful condition that the doctor said I would most likely grow out of in five or six years. Or, I could undergo surgery that *might* help but might not help the condition. The operation might also cause its own problems.

Having explained the problem to me, my parents left it to me to decide. I was seated on the front steps on a warm midsummer day in the Canadian Midwest, agonizing over the decision. In desperation, I prayed for a sign. "Please, God, if I'm not to have the operation, let me see some flowers in the sky." It was pure upsurge from my inner self. Consciously, I had no idea why I chose flowers.

Time passed. There were a few small, scattered clouds along the horizon and no breeze. Everything, it seemed, was holding its breath. From time to time, my attention wandered. Then, as the afternoon light began to change, so did the clouds. They expanded and moved closer together until they resembled – I stared at the white, pink, and mauve forms above me, with their highlights and shadows – great clusters of lilacs! I could hardly believe my eyes. I called for my mother: "Mom, look at the clouds. What do they look like to you?" She gazed briefly and said, "Why, they look like great bunches of lilacs." She did not know what I had prayed for, and I did not tell her until many years after.

I had my sign and made my decision not to have the surgery, which as it turned out later was the right decision.

The devas of the air as I understand have charge of clouds and air currents. By what wondrous series of "coincidence" did a child's earnest prayer get rerouted from "central" to their department? What was so wonderful about it was that not only the form but the colors were exactly right, and I'd had no specific flowers in mind.

Tiffany Holmes

When I was about two, I wandered away from my mother out into the middle of the street while she went on shopping. Just as a rushing truck was about to put an end to me, a woman appeared from nowhere (truly an angel of the moment), swooped me up under one arm, and headed for safety as my mother watched unaware through the store window. She didn't immediately realize that the flailing, kicking toddler under that woman's arm was her own.

Many years later when I was on a hated job, feeling sorry for myself, two things happened twenty-four hours apart. First, my boss gave me notice that Friday the thirteenth, which was two weeks away, would be my last day. Then, the next day, my agent called to say that a publisher was buying my first astrology book – allowing me to leave in a blaze of glory rather than despair.

Herb L. Rosenberg
Nevada

The angel experience I had happened when I was about four and a half years old. My sister and I were dropped off at a public pool, where she was supposed to watch me. Well, she didn't, and I jumped into the deep end of the pool. Not being able to swim, I proceeded to drown, gulping large amounts of water, trying to turn it into air. Suddenly I looked up and saw two beautiful angels floating down to get me – either to take me to God or to this life, or to both. These angels looked like Tinker Bell from Walt Disney, although they were much more ethereal.

Mary Elba Martinez
Los Angeles, California

Once when I was about seven years old my family lived in an apartment that was by itself above some garages. There was a flight of stairs with around sixteen or seventeen steps. I remember late one night I wanted to go outside and play, and my mother said no because it was too late to go outside. I became angry and stormed out the front door. I lost my balance and went flying down the steps, but to my surprise I felt two large hands holding me under my arms, and I floated down! By all rights I should have been injured badly. I remember standing at the bottom of the stairs completely petrified, yet I also felt good because something had saved me. I ran and told my mother about the incident. She believed me, but she also had negative religious beliefs about bad spirits, so I never understood what had saved me. Now I realize it was the angels.

Animal Angels and Pets

8

Robert Cole, an astrologer, points out why it makes perfect sense to honor our shared heritage with all living beings on the planet: "The latest theories of interconnectedness suggest that we all share the cells of our beings with everything else. So when I snuggle up with my cat and we purr together, the cells we share vibrate in harmonious frequency. When I marvel at the elephants in the zoo, I am truly marveling at our shared nature. When a butterfly lands on my rosebush, all three of us—the butterfly, the rosebush and myself—merge in ways which are not merely poetic. And the interconnectedness extends into time both backward into the eternal past and forward into the eternal future."

St. Francis of Assisi lived in harmony with this interconnectedness. A well-known story tells how he preached to the birds in the forest about the wonders and glory of God. A multitude of birds of all varieties came out from the trees to the ground. The birds would not leave until Francis went among them, touching them with his cloak and giving them his blessing. After he blessed them with the sign of the cross, they flew off in four directions, singing praises to God.

I have had many mystical and magical experiences with birds. One time I was sitting in a chair stuck in a negative space, and I looked over at the window and a little hummingbird was hovering in the window looking at me. As I watched him, I started laughing because of the "look" he had on his little face. He seemed to have an expression that said, Why are you taking everything so seriously, when you don't need to? I lightened up quickly, and then he moved his head and flew away. Another time I was sitting at my computer trying to write something, and nothing was coming. I just sat there *staring at the computer, getting frustrated, until I looked at the windowsill close to my left side and there was a little bird hopping around like Woodstock, Snoopy's friend. I was totally fascinated as I watched him hop back and forth on the windowsill. This experience took me completely away from the frustration. I was at one with the moment. He stopped and looked at me, turning his head from side to side as if to say good-bye, and then he flew away. Afterward I was able to write.*

Our connection with the animal world is strongest when we bond with a pet. The comfort, joy, and unconditional love a pet can bring to us is comparable to the love of the angels. As you will find in the following letters, love never dies; it only transforms and grows deeper.

Linda Kramer
Tiburon, California

When Benjamin was born on May 21, 1971, his birth marked the end of a seven-month depression for me. I had undergone thyroid surgery for a possible malignant tumor. At first I had been told that the tumor was benign, and then I was told ten days later that there were certain "suspicious" cells in the frozen section. At that time I had not yet begun my study of metaphysics, and I felt "betrayed" by my body.

Benjaperson (as he later was called in deference to the women's movement) was one of nine puppies, and I attended his birth and watched the litter grow, until at just six weeks he joined our family. He was to remain with me for the next sixteen years. I told myself that he was to be a companion for my young son; however, from the first, Benjie attached himself to me. Although he was friendly to other people, he and I were inseparable.

Benjie saw me through a dysfunctional marriage, a traumatic divorce, and my battle with rheumatoid arthritis, in which I was able to turn around a debilitating disease process to the point where I now enjoy perfect health. He was my support when I entered onto my spiritual path in 1977. No matter how much time I spent in meditation, Benjie would lie quietly under my altar. He was a constant source of strength, fun, and unconditional love.

By the time I met my husband, Hal, in 1984, Benjaperson was thirteen years old. He was still quite lively and aware, but over the next three years his health deteriorated. I, however, did not release my friend easily. I fed him large quantities of vitamins, which he ate voraciously for about a year. I took him to the vet and to alternative health practitioners. I held on for dear life. On several occasions when Benjie went into the woods and did not return home at night, Hal (at my request) and I went out and brought him home. Hal would gently try to tell me that Ben wanted to die by himself with dignity. He encouraged me by telling me that Benjie was teaching him a great lesson about dignity and death. But only when Ben himself looked at me and let me know it was time did I let him go. And so he returned home on April 5, 1987, while I meditated.

Since we had been so close, I expected that Benjie would let me know how he was doing and where he was, but for two years I could not reach him. There was nothing—no messages, no insights, no communication whatsoever. I all but gave up.

Then one day during a guided meditation, the group was

led to the celestial realm for an initiation. I entered into a large open area filled with hosts of angels. The sweet smells, soft colors, and the intense feelings of peace and joy were embodied in what seemed like hundreds of angels in traditional form. Suddenly, across the open space that separated me from the hosts, Benjaperson came running toward me. He jumped into my arms and tried to lick my face (his old earthbound ways) when suddenly I was embraced by a beautiful androgynous angel. The implication was clear to me: Benjie had been an angel all the time.

I felt pure joy at having met Ben again. And I felt humbled that such a great being as an angel would have spent sixteen earthbound years as my companion.

How can any of us ever doubt the providence of the universe, the unconditional love that is there for the asking, the beauty and the truth that are disguised in so many ordinary forms?

Name Withheld by Request

My dog Hans died two days after Operation Desert Storm began. He was killed by a car. Hans had been missing for about two days. On one of the nights (Thursday), he came to me in a dream and told me he was coming home to me. On Friday, my friends had all heard about Hans's death and knew my husband was in a wartime situation. On Saturday I received a phone call telling me that my friends Elke and Joel were at Big Star and had found a female German shepherd/hound puppy for me. The minute I heard this, I knew it was Hans's way of letting me know that he had provided companionship for me.

Her name is Courage, named for the trait I felt I needed most during the war. Hans also told me in a dream to tell my story and what I learned from it. The most valuable lesson I learned is to take no one, and nothing, for granted. Also, if God closes one door, he always opens another. I still practice those lessons today. If I can donate books that will open doors for others to read, I will. I'll surprise a friend or my doctor with candy or even a card; whatever it is—just do it. It will change both your lives. Courage is a gift from God, and she lives up to her name!

When my husband was serving in the Persian Gulf, an angel told me to turn this into a positive experience—to deal with being alone and to conquer my fears. I drove all by myself from Georgia to North Carolina to visit my mother (a three-and-a-half-hour drive), something I had never done before. My guardian angel was beside me to help and comfort me, and my mother remarked on seeing it. I know I'm going in the right direction because I'm receiving positive feedback. I'm not quite sure where I'm going though.

Patricia Flinn

New Jersey

On November 16, 1990, I lost my beloved golden retriever, O'Casey, to cancer. He was very sick for about a week and then died on our kitchen floor. Fortunately, both I and my husband, Gene, were home at the time, and we held O'Casey while he died. O'Casey was a very special animal. He used to come into the library and lie at my feet while I wrote, prayed, or meditated.

Naturally, I missed him terribly after his death and spent many a sad night grieving over him.

On the night before I discovered your book, in the bookshop in my small town, I was praying very hard to O'Casey to let him know I wished him well wherever he might be and that I wanted him back as my dog again. Around noon the following day, as I was walking toward the bookshop, I encountered a very striking woman with a beautiful golden retriever who looked very much like my O'Casey. I ran up to her and began petting the dog. In my excitement I said, "This dog is beautiful. If you ever have puppies with him, please let me know."

The woman smiled as she told me that I was indeed in luck. Her dog had fathered a litter of puppies, and there was just one left, a male puppy. From the photo she showed me, the dog looked very much like O'Casey when he was just seven weeks old. Naturally I couldn't resist. Not only did I buy your book that afternoon, but I also bought the puppy, which I like to think was sent by an angel of light named O'Casey.

Beverly Hale Watson
Florida

Pets were mentioned in your book as being sent by God. Toby was a dog of the spirit, and we had to have him put to sleep due to a disintegrating spine. The week after Toby went "home," I received a message that one day I would receive a phone call from a woman who would be moving. She would have a one-year-old silver gray poodle that she couldn't take with her. She would ask me to take him for her. I was also told by "Spirit" that when I let Toby return to his creator, he no longer was in pain and he was now free – I was to envision a lamb leaping over the clouds.

Last March, I received the foretold phone call from a total stranger. She was moving to South Carolina, and although there were two people who wanted her dog, she knew they weren't to have him. He was to be in our home. To make a long story short, we picked him up, and when he runs, he leaps like a lamb jumping over clouds!

Ellen Olender

Florida

I was at a metaphysical healing circle when the leader told us this story:

An elderly lady I know took her cat to the vet. Unfortunately, the cat needed to be put to sleep. The lady sat in the waiting room and looked out the window. She saw her cat in the arms of an angel. The angel had the face of a cat and looked at the cat with sheer love and care. Cradling the cat gently, the angel ascended. The lady watched until they were out of sight. Every time I tell this story, I get chills of affirmation.

Judith G. Zoch

Chicago, Illinois

My cat Tigrrr made his transition on April 17th – Good Friday – he was fourteen, and more human than feline. I believe he is part of another realm now, as I have received several symbolic signs to reassure me.

I was giving my boyfriend a back rub one evening, and all of a sudden a huge moth landed on his foot. It was the largest moth I've ever seen! And it's coloring and markings were exactly the same as Tigrrr's. So I believe it was his way of conveying his state of transformation. I set the moth free off the back porch; it was the fourth of July.

David L. Hays

[TLT: David is my chiropractor/healer.]

I want to share this incident, which happened during the spring of 1971 while I attended Antioch College in Yellow Springs, Ohio. I was studying the lives of John and Charles Wesley and of St. Francis of Assisi, researching the spiritual influence of these men and how they changed the course of history.

I went to the college library and asked to read a book on the legends of St. Francis that was in the rare books collection. A discussion on the advisability of letting me read such a rare book ensued, when the wife of a professor I knew overheard the discussion and, realizing it was me, came out and vouched for my character. So I was given the book to read in the library.

I sat down at a desk facing a south window, when a "street" tomcat strode into the library, as if he owned the place, pointedly ignoring the sign stating "NO ANIMALS ALLOWED." He walked straight down the middle of the corridor to where I was sitting, jumped onto my lap, and promptly fell asleep. My whole nervous system was electrified while I read the rare book from cover to cover that afternoon, as the cat slept peacefully on my lap. When I finished, I told the cat that I wanted to move, and he clearly conveyed to me his annoyance at my interrupting his nap. He leaped down and disdainfully walked out of the library, allowing no one to touch him. I assumed St. Francis sent the cat. You may assume it was angels or both. In my practice, I have had many incidents of invisible helpers while treating patients. For example, a phone rings, no one is there, and the patient gets better without me touching him or her. Thank you for your book; it was a gentle reminder for me to acknowledge the spiritual hierarchy, the healing angels, and the healing devas.

Joan P. Lockwood
Pennsylvania

I bought a pair of zebra finches Saturday night, and I angelically named them Raphael and Gabriel. I was very upset to find Gabriel dead on Tuesday morning. I was glad to find Raphael was the picture of health. I was trying to get the gumption to gather up Gabriel to return to the pet store in exchange for a new bird and decided to prolong the agony by getting the mail first. I was very pleasantly surprised to find your newsletter, and the St. Raphael prayer card fell from the envelope and landed near the bird cage. Ironically enough, it was the same angel card I had given my sister two weeks prior, to protect her newborn daughter who was being transferrred via helicopter to a speciality hospital for possible open heart surgery, not even twenty-four hours after being born. My niece had a very safe trip, and miraculously her condition reversed itself. She returned safely home in perfect health after umpteen tests all returned negative. She is fine today, as is Michael Gabriel, my newest finch.

Sharon Jackson
San Jose, California

I was in my backyard watering, feeling sorry for myself after a trying situation with my son – in general just feeling miserable – when I was touched by the angel clan. All of a sudden, a beautiful sprite of a hummingbird flew about two feet from me and hovered, looking at me. He flew through the water spray, turned, and flew through again. He looked at me again. He repeated his dash through the "hose rain" and hovered again, looking at me. He then flew to my clothesline to shake off and clean his feathers. I felt filled to the brim with the message of care and love and hope! I cried uncontrollably – what a blessing I was just given! My problem seemed so insignificant. When I think of my "friend," my heart soars. There are so many beings, other than human, who truly love us and try to help us when we ask. I also know the feelings that emanate from our brother/sister trees, bushes, and so on. They truly care and are asking us to wake up!

Nancy Grimley Carleton
Berkeley, California

Since writing a piece on animal angels for the Angel Forum in *Messengers of Light*, I have received several dozen letters and calls from people around the country. Many of these people had recently lost a dearly beloved animal friend who they felt might be an angel. Most asked how to handle the terrible grief surrounding the loss.

Here I offer some answers I hope will prove helpful to those who have lost animal friends. These suggestions come from a variety of sources, including my training as a psychotherapist and my experience in meditating on angels. I have had to put these suggestions into practice in the past year, because of the death of Willow, the rabbit I wrote about in *Messengers of Light*. He died the day after Easter in 1991, following a long and agonizing illness. The loving spirit with which he faced his illness and met his death only reconfirmed for me his angelic essence.

If you, too, have lost a beloved animal, my first words to you are: Be gentle with yourself. Allow your grief to move through you. Let the tears come, and let them cleanse you. As you allow the grief to flow through you, you may hear the echoes of earlier losses. You may move through the stages of denial, bargaining, anger, and depression before you reach the stage of acceptance. Let yourself experience all of this. The more you can open to the process, the greater the healing you will receive.

Give yourself space to grieve. If you can, take some time off work. Set aside some time each day to meditate or pray. Rituals offer an opportunity to express gratitude for the gift of your animal friend's presence in your life and to call on the wisdom of whatever spiritual tradition speaks to your heart. Light a candle for your animal friend, and ask the angels to watch over and receive him or her. Put fresh flowers on the grave or at the spot where your animal loved to bask in the sun. Repeat this process on significant anniversaries or whenever you feel moved to connect with your animal friend.

Not all in our society understand the depth and spirit animals bring to our lives. When you've lost an animal friend, be sure to share your feelings with people in your life who have also connected deeply with animals. You may find it valuable to seek out a therapist, counselor, or spiritual adviser to help you through the grief process. Ask the angels to help guide you to one who truly understands about animals.

Many people find they have some "unfinished business" to deal with as they go through the grief process. Many letters I received expressed some kind of guilt. Consider writing a letter or letters to your animal friend expressing your feelings; ask the angels to deliver it. Apologize for any ways you feel you weren't able to give all you would have liked, and ask for forgiveness. Listen for the answer. If you open your heart, your animal friend will bless you with forgiveness and acceptance. Follow that example, and forgive yourself.

Spend some extra time giving comfort to your inner child. Our inner child is the part of us that connects most deeply with animals, and the part of us that most needs the unconditional love they give us. Visualize your adult self loving and comforting your inner child. Remind your inner child that you can still talk to your animal friend in your heart.

Recognize that your animal friend came to teach you about unconditional love and about opening your heart. That unconditional love still exists; it is part of who you are. Surround yourself with reminders of that great love of which we are all part; these reminders may take the form of photos of your animal friend, pictures of angels, favorite meditation passages, or beautiful objects from nature.

When you're ready, open your heart to receive love from new animal friends. Around the time Willow died, I had been taking care of a rabbit named Nutmeg for a friend. Willow loved Nutmeg, and she brightened his final days. After Willow's death, Nutmeg launched a very deliberate campaign to become a member of my household. Initially, I resisted – the grief was too fresh – but eventually her love and persistence melted my heart, and my friend allowed her to stay with me. Later that year, Nutmeg wove a spell around me (I know no other way to put it), and I found myself bringing home a mate for her. Soon after Blackberry joined our household, Nutmeg, a very determined rabbit who always knows what she wants, achieved her next goal – motherhood. So now I have the company of six sweet rabbits, including the babies – Parsley, Juniper, Hazel, and Shasta – who are now fully grown. Although none can ever replace Willow, each brings to my life a unique expression of joy, love, and spirit. And each day I am aware of the continuing presence of Willow, who serves as a generous, loving guardian watching over me and my new rabbit family.

Creative Angel Promptings

9

The angels are creativity ministers. They love to attend to the human need for personal creative expression. Creativity blesses all of us; we all have an inner child who longs to color a picture with crayons. In the following letters, people share ways the angels inspired them to let their own special creativity loose.

Star Light Mail
Colorado

My friend and I have started an angel light mail altar especially for angel mail/requests. The altar is filled with crystals, a burning candle of pink, white (or whatever light color we're inspired to use), along with rose or cedar incense and a small bell—all in a sunny window facing east. We put the larger crystals on top of the unopened envelopes. I am in the process of making a light mailbox to put on the altar. All the light mail stays on the altar for about one cycle of the moon—depending on when it reaches us. Then the mail is burned in a quiet, wooded area by a brook during the full moon.

If you would like to send any of your requests or letters through our angel altar, we'd be more than happy to pray over them and add them to ours! The angel mail remains unopened (by us) unless there is an "O" on the back flap of the envelope. We lay hands on top of the envelopes each morning with an affirmation, such as: "Divine love works on these for the highest good of all concerned. May the angels be blessed as we have been blessed. May these requests travel at light-speed and be answered at the speed of light. So be it!" We're having a lot of fun with this; it has made our hearts light!

Terry Lynn Taylor

I was so impressed with the creative approach of Star Light Mail that I asked "Star" if she would like to list her prayer service in my newsletter. I have seen immediate prayer intercession change moments of despair into moments of divine comfort. I was not only impressed by the creativity of Star's offer, but with the generous spiritual gift it was giving people. Star said she would like a listing in the newsletter and it read as follows:

A very special person has offered readers of the newsletter the chance to send prayer requests in for empowerment on her special angel altar, through her prayer service: Star Light Mail. She started Star Light Mail by putting friends' notes, letters, or pictures on her angel altar. She would burn incense, light a candle, and then converse, pray, meditate, hold a conference with, and/or visualize the angels for an hour each morning, usually between 7:00 and 8:00 A.M. After a month of prayer, unless requested otherwise, she burns the requests (not photos) at an allowed area in a quiet wooded park. She feels the angels playing, laughing, and singing around her as she burns the requests. The positive energy released in the flames of the prayers keeps her feeling joyful and energized for hours afterward. So if you have a special request you would like her to energize with the angels, send it to Star Light Mail. She mentioned that some people send a photo for healing (she doesn't burn the photos), and she asks that you please put an address on the back, and she will return all photos sent. If anyone has suggestions for prayer network(play)ing, let her know. Thank you, Star Light Mail; this is a very powerful way to share the light of God!

A few weeks later I received this note from Star:

I have received about twelve letters so far in response to your mention of Star Light Mail in Angels Can Fly. Every two to three days, I check the post office box and get another couple of prayer requests. They come from all over the states. So far, pretty amazing and very humbling. Some days I have to be at work by 8:00 A.M., so I get up an hour earlier to play/pray with the angels over the prayer requests. I feel so "charged up" by this now! It's like spiritual exercise—"angel aerobics" if you will! Truly wonderful! Thanks again for the mention of Star Light Mail.

[TLT: Star Light Mail's address is P.O. Box 4271, Boulder, CO 80306.]

Christina L. Ross

North Carolina

I'm having a very angelic month! Something happened to me last night and I'm hoping you can help me figure out what it was.

About an hour before I went to bed, I was doing something "light" to help me sleep. I was making an angel scrapbook, which I dedicated to my guardian angel, Annabelle. She appeared before me once, and she is beautiful. I made this book to thank her. In it are poems about angels, pictures of angels, something I wrote about Namaste, and the prayer to St. Raphael with the angel card picture you sent of him. It's delightful! My daughters, Katie and Amy, love the scrapbook and want to make one, too.

In the last two pages is a picture of the archangel Uriel, leader of the seraphim. It is a print of an oil painted by Pietro Cavallini called "The Last Judgment." On the page next to the print, I wrote, "To honor the archangel URIEL, highest of the seraphim." His six wings are breathtaking! After finishing the scrapbook, I went to bed and fell asleep on my stomach. In the middle of the night, I was awakened by the most tremendous "blast" of energy I have ever felt. I meditate often, and my spiritual guides give me energy and spine cleanings. But this was unlike any-thing I have ever felt! It hit me square in the back like a bolt of lightning, but it didn't hurt, of course. I raised my head, and the whole bedroom was lit with all the colors of alabaster and beau-tiful white light. The energy traveled down my spine in both directions – rushing to my tailbone and bursting into my skull. I'll never forget this feeling. Do you have any idea what hap-pened? My first thought was, it's a thank-you gift from Uriel; he got my message.

Isabel Victoria

Sohaven Retreat, Florida

Letter 1

I'd like to share some angel fun with you. Sohaven is a retreat in the hills of Florida, totally dedicated to the play of angels and devas. We have a Sunday healing/prayer circle that has been playing with the angels for two years now. Let me tell you some of the wonderful games the angels have taught us.

Angelgrams: Angelgrams are similar to the angel mail you wrote about in *Messengers of Light*. Our method is to use huge art paper. If we wish to release stuff, we write what we wish to release. Then we draw, paint, and splash an angel over each item and ask the angel to handle it. Then we burn it, so that we are *really* letting it go! Angelgrams are also used for sending things to other people, such as prosperity, healing, creativity, or "just" joy. We address the angels of the particular person, for example, "To Alan David's Angels." Then we write what that person needs in the "I am" format: "I am prosperous; I am creative," and so forth. Then we do our angel drawings for this — one or two big angels or lots of little ones, whichever feels like the most fun at the moment. Then we burn them with great thanksgiving. We are all doing them so often for each other that we rarely need to do one for ourselves! And it is so much nicer and more fun to do one for someone else. People who are the most sensitive in the group can feel when one is being done for them. They say they feel peace rushing in around them and an urge to smile.

Another fun thing we have been given is *angel halo energizing*. We stand face-to-face with a partner and take turns. First I ask to borrow Alan's highest angel's halo. I hold my hands over his head until I feel the halo being placed in my hands. Then I allow it to expand till it will go around him. I lower it down over his head and shoulders, lowering it down slowly to the floor. If there is a blockage, the halo will get stuck to try to clear it. Then it will go on; it will also slow down if healing is needed in the area. (We find it getting stuck most often in the heart area.) We do angel halo energizing three times from head to toe, then place the halo on top of the person's head and then thank the angel. Those in the group who are clairvoyant can see the halo turn colors. It's always golden when it is handed to us. The colors we see the most often are all shades of violet and blue, and some rose and orange. We figure these are colors the people need in their auras. We take turns doing this to teach that *everyone* can work (play) with the angels.

I belong to the legions of Metatron, and my partner, Alan, is one of Michael's charges. We fluff each other's wings and those of anyone else who will hold still for it. Oh, I almost forgot— this is good! We got rid of deerflies on our ten acres by writing an angelgram to the deva of the deerflies! It took three angel-grams, but it worked. Now that is something you can point to!

Letter 2

The main idea here is to spread angelic vibrations. We are always up to something new, and every time the angels give us a new idea, we tell everybody!

The angels gave one of our healers a great new gift last week (at a flea market)—a set of twelve tiny bells on a string. She tin-kles it over the "healer" on the table, and we can hear the angels flutter and giggle. Before we brought the angels into our prac-tices, we used to do a ten-minute prayer/meditation circle, with hands-on healing and absentee healings. Now it takes fifteen to twenty minutes, because someone in the circle always bursts out laughing, especially at the point when I ask people to merge with their angels. But it sure does raise the vibrations!

One day I had been mining crystals and came home very

tired. My partner, who was with me, was very sore and asked for a massage. I was too tired to oblige, so as I passed out I sent a silent prayer to Raphael: "Please fix my friend! I'm just too tired to help." Then I was gone. The next morning, my friend woke up amazed that there was no muscle soreness and told me his dream of that night. "A huge green person picked me up and manipulated my whole body! It seemed to last about an hour!" Dream? I think not; I just said, "Thanks, Raphael."

Because of our angelic origin, we are all really angels-in-training (relearning). Tell your people to sit quietly and ask for their *angel names* so that they can use them often for peaceful empowerment. Mine is Lil Lea Aiel. It is important to trust what you first hear and write it down. After you have begun using the name, you can ask questions, such as "What does it mean?" I believe we all used these angel names in our first physical incarnation. When people in our group get their angel names, we have them draw their concept of an angel and put their angel names on them. Then we hang them on a special empty wall in the healing room. Yes, it looks like a young mom's ice box, but we love it!

Chris Cox

Maryland

I have established a large corkboard (36″×48″) as an angel and goal board. I have one chief angel who helps all the other angels in their respective tasks, as well as helps the angels combine all their activities to be supportive of my ultimate spiritual direction. There are eight other angels, whom I have assigned

161

a number of areas in my life, such as healing, love, gratitude, forgiveness, positive thinking, peace of mind, and so on. I have based the idea on Napoleon Hill's book *You Can Work Your Own Miracles,* in which he has a chapter entitled "Our Unseen Guides." He mentions his "Eight Guiding Princes" who have helped him enormously in his life. He has his own ideas as to the nature of these guides, as do the many successful men he quotes, but it matters not. What does matter is that help is available for all those who have faith in the system and are willing to take their assistance in gratitude and thanksgiving.

Tina Ryan
Staten Island, New York

I'd like you to know that many months ago I started what I call an "angel wall" – a collection of different angels that I find in the many catalogs I receive. It's coming along slowly. I have plaques, pictures, and statues of angels, which I enjoy looking at. My grandson recently gave me an angel pin. I had a perm and noticed the beautician had the same pin. There are many of us!

Tiffany Holmes

[TLT: Tiffany is an astrologer and has come up with a unique way to do an angel conference. I discuss the angel conference in Mes-sengers of Light; it is a method for calling upon the angels to help

you turn over certain issues for divine transmutation. I use a divided circle on paper with a section for each issue. I then assign an angel to the issue and pick an ANGEL® card for insight and answers about how to deal with the issue.]

The twelve-house circle structure is familiar to those who've read any astrology and can be applied to readings of all spreadable oracles having twelve or more pieces. A circle, in general, is the symbol of completeness. The form is satisfying, as it covers all facets of human experience. The questions below indicate the subject matter covered by each house, but should not be adopted unless they truly fit your situation. Basically, these are simply hints that can be reworded to reflect your present circumstances and wishes. Following the question for the house is a brief listing of the [other] subjects represented by that house, as a further guidance for understanding and wording of your questions. Don't expect all meanings of each house to be equally important to you at any given time. For each house and question, you can pick an ANGEL® card or any other oracle piece. The traditional astrological circle is divided into the twelve equal sections in the following ways, using reference to the clock dial. At 9:00 is house number one, 8:00 is house number two, and so on until you reach house twelve, which corresponds to 10:00. The questions and related issues are as follows for the houses:

1. How can I improve my energy level and general well-being? Related issues: the self, ego, physical body, vitality, demeanor, temperament.
2. How can I improve my assets and my use of time? Related issues: possessions, money, attitude toward posses-

sions, and management of time – the most important possession of all.

3. How can I improve my intellect, my state of mind, and my writing? Related issues: mental/educational development, short journeys, relationships with neighbors, cousins, and siblings.

4. How can I improve my home? Related issues: the home, base of operations.

5. How can I get more fun into my life? Related issues: risks of all kinds, including love, sex, procreation, the stock market, games of chance, show business, creativity in general, pleasure and vacations.

6. How can I improve the performance of my work? Related issues: the manner in which duties are performed, relationships with coworkers and subordinates, diet and health, the role of disorders in our lives.

7. How can I improve my already-good relationship with my mate? Related issues: relationships of equals, spouses, partners, collaborators, advisers, clients, competitors, and open enemies.

8. How can I better reduce my debt balance and gain my financial freedom? Related issues: debts – both material and moral; the expectations we have of others; taxes and legacies; attitudes toward death; last-minute angel rescues.

9. How can I improve my outlook? Related issues: philosophical/religious beliefs, long-distance travel, public forums such as the media and the courts.

10. How can I improve my career and the esteem in which I am held? Related issues: career, honor or disgrace, the opinions of those who don't know us personally.

11. How can I improve my friendships? Related issues: friends, acquaintances, attitudes toward friendship, social concerns, wishes and dreams.
12. How can I enrich my time alone or doing solitary pursuits in my mate's presence? Related issues: solitude, privacy, retreat, things unseen.

Joanna Schohl
Wisconsin

This past month, while sitting through a rather dry sermon in church, a thought came to me very clearly: "Have a special evening on the angels." I became very excited about the whole prospect, and a friend and I decided to host a spiritual gathering on the angels. We chose December 14 as the date, and we invited about a dozen guests—friends who we knew would be interested in learning more about the angels and acknowledging their presence in our lives.

We bathed our living room in candlelight and Christmas tree lights, and set out various pictures and likenesses of angels that we had collected. When our friends arrived, many had brought a special angel of theirs to share with the group as we had suggested on the invitations. We began by singing "Hark the Herald Angels Sing," and then took time for each person to tell a little bit about the angels she had brought and to pass them around the gathering. We then heard some Christmas Bible readings about angels, and talked about memories we each had about angels when we were children and now. Discussion also focused on the roles angels have in relation to human beings and our spirituality. My friend then shared a few ideas from *Messengers of Light*. We sang "Angels We Have Heard on High," and then did a group meditation with the ANGEL® cards; we all picked cards after formulating a question/concern within our-selves. We ended by singing angelic Christmas carols together. I must add that we also had fun devising tasty and pertinent refreshments—including a light pink holiday punch, chocolate-covered angel food candy, and angel cutout cookies—all served by candlelight. Even the round snack crackers passed as "halos" to some!

Many of the people who came said they felt deep peace and serenity throughout the evening. When I woke up the morn-ing of the gathering, I smiled, as I had a very clear sense that our house was "stuffed with angels." I sense that there were many pleased and joyous angelic spirits here that night! It was a peace-ful and holy evening. The angels were present and tending to our hearts in their usual playful and "lightsome" way.

Terry Lynn Taylor

I'm always glad to hear of people who want to start an angel group or have a special gathering to bring the angels closer to their hearts. In response to requests asking what I do during an angel gathering, I quickly made a list of some sug-gestions. You don't need a lot of people for an angel group. I would say anywhere from three to fifteen is great. One of my favorite gatherings was a circle of eight women including my-self. A special bonding occurred among us, and I feel it partly happened because, one, we were all women and, two, the number eight represents infinity, and a circle never ends. Of course, I have thoroughly enjoyed each and every time I have gathered with people in the name of the angels, and men are always welcome.

A couple of things to think about in setting up an angel group: One of the basic reasons angels are available for us is to awaken the Christ light within. So it is good to acknowledge and thank God for your personal spiritual helpers. Jesus said in Matthew 18:19–20: "Again I say to you, that if two of you agree on earth about anything that you may ask, it shall be done for you by my Father who is in heaven, for where two or three have gathered together in my name there I am in their midst." Gathering together is a sure way to attract many angels. Here are some additional ideas:

1. Make sure you have some white candles burning; you may use other colors, too—just be sure at least one of the candles is white. If you have a way of scenting the air with natural flower essences, do so. Burning subtle incense clears and cleanses the air. Burning it beforehand will help in case someone is allergic. Create an angel focus center (altar), with fresh flowers, an angel figurine or picture, other sacred items that inspire you, and a burning candle.

2. I always start my angel talks by asking people to take a few moments to go into a semimeditative state and allow their minds to come up with an image or thought or visualization about an angel. I tell them to let their minds go freely with the thought of what angels mean to them without preconceived ideas. In other words, they may just experience

a feeling, see a quick image flash by, or hear something. After a few moments, go around the circle (I always have people sit in a circle) and ask each person to share his or her experience. Then discuss similarities and differences, feelings and images, and so forth.

3. Discuss new books about angels, articles people have read, and any current angel news. Share journal ideas, prayers, spiritual tools, and any creative inspiration the angels have brought your way that could inspire others.

4. Of course, it's a natural to share angel experiences people have had currently or in their past. This usually happens on its own.

5. Always allow room for spontaneous ideas to flow. Let the angels guide you. Even if you have prepared a certain agenda, the angels may lead you somewhere else. Keep unused ideas for other times.

6. Sometimes an angel meeting is simply a time to share personal feelings about our spiritual paths. It is good to get feedback on spiritual dilemmas. If the group goes this way, and if it is clear people want feedback, remind everyone to practice unconditional acceptance and allow people's angel guides to help those wanting feedback.

7. If someone in the group wants help in healing an ailment or negative pattern, have the circle join hands and ask all present to ask their guardian angels to assist the person's guardian angel in pouring angelic light from God into the person's life or onto the area needing healing. Ask all present to visualize the light and open their hearts to the angelic vibrations of love coming from the realm of God–heaven–and for them to accept healing also for themselves.

These days it seems to be difficult for people to be consistent in attending group meetings. I hope this changes; we need one another in our own spiritual and personal growth.

Clara Utter

Norwich, New York

Angel Trainers Meeting

When: 7:00 P.M. every other Tuesday night.

Object: Fun; discussing angels and angelic happenings; networking for others in group; spirituality.

Opening: Lord's Prayer and prayer to the archangel Michael for protection. Looking for good things happening to people each week. How to bring angels closer to us.

Closing: "I believe in God. I believe in angels. I believe angels are the messengers of God. They transfer our prayers and God's answers for us. For their endeavors on our behalf, we thank them very much. We ask God to bless each of us and them through the weeks ahead that we may regather in the spirit of joy. Amen."

Poetry

The poetry of heaven's love joins friends in common rhyme
and speaks with every syllable of bonds that have no time.
Author unknown; contributed by Nancy C. Miles

Mary F. Downey

Port Washington, New York

I was moved to write a poem for you with Raphael's card sitting right in front of me. I've enclosed it, and I also have a writing tool to share with you: I've just returned to working on my first novel, after having let it go for three years, due to fear and self-doubt. In order to write joyously, I create a joyous space around me. On my writing table, I have flowers, four little angel figurines, and an amethyst crystal, and I spray the air with floral perfume. I wear a flowered kimono, instead of the usual sweatshirt! I am thus surrounded by beauty. Before I begin writing, I repeat an affirmation from Louise Hay: "I am an open channel for divine ideas to flow through me, and the creativity of the universe now expresses through me. That which I need to know is revealed to me, and whatever I need comes to me. I am divinely protected and guided, and my way is made smooth and easy." These rituals clear a space for inspired, joyful writing. Raphael's poem:

To Raphael, For Spring, With Love

The earth stirred from her soft, still sleep
And, awakened, stretched leafy arms in joy,
As Raphael shot green grassy arrows through her heart.
Heavenly hued spirits joined the dance, masquerading as
    flowers.

As angelic aromas caress the air,
I, too, am moved to laugh and play—
Wear a silly straw hat with cherries on the brim,
Put on shocking pink eyeshadow,
Raise my hemline three inches,
Be a wondrous April fool.

Dear Raphael, shining spirit of spring,
You gave my soul a song to sing.
As the bluebells blossomed and the bluebirds pealed,
My heart whispered, "God has healed."

Lori Jean Flory
Colorado

Where Angels Dance

Feel us, see us, hear us, echoing your beauty,
We gracefully move across the essence of your soul,
For we are you—you are we.

Feel us dance, feel us move, like the ballet dancers of your love.
Of the poise, the grace, your soul is within.

Feel us hover through the air all around you.
We tousle your hair, feel your ears, and bestow a kiss on
   the face—
Like a breeze brushing your cheek with gentleness, love,
   and compassion.

Answers From the Angels

Dance with us, move to the music, flow with us, feel your
    body of light, and forget the physical.
Flow, it is only us in the room with you.
Seen and unseen.

Let your aura radiate bright; let your joy sparkle.
Improvise as you go along and we shall inspire you.
Let your arms flow and your feet follow a path all their
    own.
You are music. You are we.

Feel your translucent robes of light move and flow as your
    dance evolves.
You are the gift. Accept it [you].
Feel the hair of your light body flow and shine.

Let us lift and twirl you,
Allow the robes of light to flare gracefully as you move on
    your own stage.
We shall take your hand lightly in ours, to free and sup-
    port you in your expression.

For we dance continuously around you, playing up and
    down.
We are the dance of joy, of love.
Join us and be one of us.
Let go.
– The Angels.

Beverly Hale Watson
North Carolina

Guardian Angels

Guardian angels up in the sky —
Heavenly protection they provide.
Assigned to us upon our birth,
They remain 'til we depart the earth.

Forever standing by our sides,
In their care we do abide.
Cherubim and seraphim, experienced they must be!
Yet totally invisible they are to you and me.

When danger rears its ugly head
And you're alive . . . instead of dead,
Praise these angels from on high,
Who keep you safe by day and night.

No reason should you be afraid
For God provides our every need.
With angels watching o'er us
To them our lives he has in trust.

Mechel Cisco
Georgia

Glistening Wings

Sweet and sleepy, the night stands still.
Moonbeams fall on my windowsill.
You come by glistening wings,
Your smile as warm as the days of spring.
You gently touch my cheek so fair
With fingertips light and soft as air.
On stardust, you bend to one knee,
Sweetly you whisper, "Oh how loved thou be."
Off unto the stars you then fly away.
As I wait for the end of a new day.

Salanda (Sa-lawn-dah)
Oregon

Thank the Angels That Be

Every day now more I know
   as my heart continues to me show

That a life lived without trust
   will soon be found in negative rust.

With each moment are opportunities
to grow, to know of the angels' glees.

They're patiently waiting just around,
waiting as we each break new ground.

They have divine purposes to serve;
as friends they'll not throw us a curve.

They closely fit every human need
as we reckon with life and then heed.

There're angels who heal or reveal
as human heart's appetite seeks meal.

Angels of love match human hearts,
work wonders daily as love imparts.

Angels also copilot our journeys;
without them, we lack life's glees.

Angels of joy, prosperity, guardianship abound
as moments where negativity's not found.

Angels bring many miracles to pass,
but many of us humans deny it all, alas.

If you're in need of an uplifting steed,
call on the angel of the need's like creed.

There's an angel hosting every purpose,
   serving good of all concerned, love's exodus.

They wait our honest beckoned call,
   wishing for us our hearts to stand tall.

I'll not stop asking help from them;
   I know life without them's pretty slim.

I thank all the angels among us that be,
   assisting my soul now free through eternity.

Carol J. Coyer
Wisconsin

   This poem is very special to me, and I would love to be able to share it with as many people as possible. I also have a special angel request, and it is that more people become aware of the plight of the homeless and hungry among us. But for the grace of God any of us could be in their shoes.

Angel of Light

A visitor came in the dark of night,
A radiant presence, with countenance bright.

In a voice as crisp, and clear as a bell,
My mission on earth she proceeded to tell.

176

"Awake from your dreams my sleepy one,
For time is short, there's much work to be done."

"The poor need clothing, the hungry must be fed,
Arise my child from your warm cozy bed."

"Go into the streets and alleyways,
Where your homeless brothers spend their days."

"Share what you have," I was told,
"It will be returned one hundredfold."

As she knelt by my bedside, and silently prayed,
Her lovely presence began to fade.

I arose from my bed with a change of heart,
Ready and willing to do my part.

Renaté Maria Bell
Lake Mary, Florida

Angels of the Kingdom

Angels of the kingdom,
High above our world,
Circle with opened wings
In faithful protection,

177

Coming to our side,
To keep our feet grounded,
To maintain our peace,
To guide in our growth,
To lend a hand if weak.
They stay busy at work,
Looking for a victory
Throughout every day.
It is reassuring to know
That the light from above
Shines down to us
to light our lifelong paths
With love and concern,
Radiating from the circle
Of glowing white light,
And the felt presence within their angelic aura.
As the angels of the kingdom
Work to harmonize the earth,
We, weaker ones below,
Should give thanks
To their daily assistance.

Barb Martin

Wisconsin

I'm sending my two short bursts of angel rhyme in addition to another poem. This is a rather big departure for me; I mean to send simple poems, but I wanted you to know how much "angelness" has filled my head.

Creative Angel Promptings

An angel takes my hand each day
   and leads me forward, out to play.
He whispers, and my mind takes flight;
   I know that what he says is "right."
Then laughter starts to fill my soul;
   My dreams, my wishes are his goal.
He says there will no limit be
   if I but bid him bide with me.

❀

I held a burden in my life,
   my thoughts and actions dwelt in strife.
I said and pondered all my woe,
   in deep despair, nowhere to go.
Then suddenly, I felt her touch
   and heard her say, "You're loved so much!"
She taught me then about my worth
   while deftly planting seeds of mirth.
My spirit rose with each new day,
   and finally I learned to play.
Then, while I played, I "felt" two more,
   and greater joy was yet in store.
The angels told me they were there
   in answer to my heartfelt prayer.
And all I had to do was ask,
   and they would aid in every task.
My woe is now replaced with love
   by angel blessings from above.

Today

Dear Heavenly Father, I ask for your help
  In guiding my "thought-steps" today.
Bring laughter and joy and compassion to me
  As I journey along life's new day.
Please help me abide in a oneness with you
  And in all things see *you* are near,
That each breath I take is a blessing you make,
  And it's *you* in each sound that I hear.
Enfold me in angels from morning through night,
  Who'll teach me each step of the way
To know each event has been heaven-sent,
  And I've walked with you all through this day.

Alonzo Leon Rhames
Arizona

Sometimes

There is a space between the moon and the sun
Which nothing ever touches—
A space where the heart and the mind are born,
Unhampered by man's smallness, his possessiveness,
His fears, or his prejudices.
This is the place where all peoples meet as one.
Their light is the stars; their warmth,
The heavens around them.

180

Their hearts are connected as one,
And their minds are free.
All things live in the light, which is Love;
Its energy, understanding.
This is the place where time neither moves
Nor exists.
This is the place of our dreams.

Dear Readers:

Please write if you would like to find out more about the people mentioned in the book who are actively promoting angel consciousness, by way of seminars, consultations, publications, and so forth.

The *Angels Can Fly* newsletter is sent out at the beginning of each season. One goal of the newsletter is to focus on the angelic energy of the particular season and to offer ideas and tools for expanding one's own angel consciousness. For a sample copy of *Angels Can Fly,* please write:

Terry Lynn Taylor
Angels Can Fly
2275 Huntington Dr., #326
San Marino, CA 91108

I am currently collecting accounts of children's experiences with angels and spirit guides.

ANGEL® cards are available in many metaphysical bookstores. If you would like to order them by mail, contact:

Music Design
1845 N. Farwell Ave.
Milwaukee, WI 53202
1 (800) 862-7232

Retail or wholesale orders are accepted. ANGEL® cards are now available in French, German, and Spanish as well as English.

COMPATIBLE BOOKS

FROM H J KRAMER INC

MESSENGERS OF LIGHT:
THE ANGELS' GUIDE TO SPIRITUAL GROWTH
by Terry Lynn Taylor
At last, a practical way to connect with the
angels and to bring heaven into your life!

GUARDIANS OF HOPE:
THE ANGELS' GUIDE TO PERSONAL GROWTH
by Terry Lynn Taylor
GUARDIANS OF HOPE *brings the angels*
down to earth with over sixty angel practices.

WAY OF THE PEACEFUL WARRIOR
by Dan Millman
A tale of transformation and adventure . . .
a worldwide best-seller.

SACRED JOURNEY OF THE PEACEFUL WARRIOR
by Dan Millman
"After you've read SACRED JOURNEY, you will know
what possibilities await you." — WHOLE LIFE TIMES

NO ORDINARY MOMENTS
by Dan Millman
Based on the premise that we can change our world by
changing ourselves, Dan shares an approach to life that turns
obstacles into opportunities and experiences into wisdom.

An Orin/DaBen Book
CREATING MONEY
by Sanaya Roman and Duane Packer, Ph.D.
This best-selling book teaches advanced manifesting techniques.

TALKING WITH NATURE
by Michael J. Roads
"From Australia comes a major new writer . . . a magnificent book!"
— RICHARD BACH, Author, *Jonathan Livingston Seagull*

JOURNEY INTO NATURE
by Michael J. Roads
"If you only read one book this year, make that book
JOURNEY INTO NATURE." — FRIEND'S REVIEW

SIMPLE IS POWERFUL
by Michael J. Roads
Embarking on a search for meaning and freedom in their lives,
Michael and Treenie discover that answers are often deceptively simple.

COMPATIBLE BOOKS

FROM H J KRAMER INC

THE EARTH LIFE SERIES
by Sanaya Roman
A course in learning to live with joy,
sense energy, and grow spiritually.

LIVING WITH JOY, BOOK I
"I like this book because it describes the way I feel
about so many things." —VIRGINIA SATIR

PERSONAL POWER THROUGH AWARENESS:
A GUIDEBOOK FOR SENSITIVE PEOPLE, BOOK II
"Every sentence contains a pearl. . . ." —LILIAS FOLAN

SPIRITUAL GROWTH:
BEING YOUR HIGHER SELF, BOOK III
Orin teaches how to reach upward to align with the
higher energies of the universe, look inward to expand
awareness, and move outward in world service.

IN SEARCH OF BALANCE
by John Robbins and Ann Mortifee
An inquiry into issues and concerns of the heart from
the best-selling author of DIET FOR A NEW AMERICA.

UNDERSTAND YOUR DREAMS
by Alice Anne Parker
A practical book that offers the reader
the key to dream interpretation.

THE COMPLETE HOME GUIDE TO AROMATHERAPY
by Erich Keller
An easy-to-use guide to aromatherapy that opens
the door to the magical world of natural scents.

WHEN FAIRY TALE ROMANCES BREAK REAL HEARTS
by Kimberley Heart
A guide to creating loving lasting relationships using proven
methods for making real and sustainable life changes.

THE WIZDOM WITHIN
by Susan Jean and Dr. Irving Oyle
"Fascinating! Illuminating . . .
Reading this book can be hazardous to your preconceptions."
—WILLIS HARMON, President, Institute of Noetic Sciences